STALWART

Naval Journeys of E. J. Ridgeway
Gunner's Mate First Class
on the
USS *Vincennes* (CA-44)
and
USS *Santa Fe* (CL-60)
1940-1946

Author, Dale J. Ridgeway

STALWART

Naval Journeys of E. J. Ridgeway

Gunner's Mate First Class

on the

USS *Vincennes* (CA-44) and USS *Santa Fe* (CL-60)

1940-1946

Copyright © 2016 by Dale J. Ridgeway

Cover Page Designed by:

Banner Digital and Publishing, Inc.

167 Citation Court

Birmingham, AL 35209

205-942-2071

www.bannerdigitalprintingandpublishing.com

ISBN – 978-0-87121-125-5 (Paperback)

ACKNOWLEDGEMENTS

My father, E. J. Ridgeway, rarely talked about his remarkable war years in the Pacific. Discovering this part of his life, which is a testimony to his fighting spirit, was quite the adventure. Thank you, Dad, for leaving such a legacy for your family.

Dad's nephew, Llewellyn "Lew" Painter, served on the escort carrier, USS *Fanshaw Bay*, among the crew of the courageous Taffy 3 Unit at the Battle off Samar (Leyte Gulf Operation). Thank you, Lew, for your muster and bravery in one of the most remarkable fights in the Pacific Theater. For most of his life after the war, Lew consistently lobbied Washington, D.C. requesting that his Uncle E. J. be awarded the Purple Heart for his injuries at the Battle of Savo Island.

Without the support and dedication of my wife, Janice, this book would not have been possible. Janice worked countless hours plowing through my "vomit" draft and developed it into a working manuscript. Thank you, Janice, for your love, patience and support.

The input of Dr. John Killian, long-time friend and confidant, encouraged me to bring this project to its conclusion. Thank you, John, for validating Dad's war story as one that should be told.

TABLE OF CONTENTS

PROLOGUE

Two young sailors dressed in crisp, white uniforms stood, one at each end of my father's coffin, while a third blew taps. The sailors removed the United States Flag that draped the casket, folded it into the official triangle, and handed it to my mother. I watched them raise their eyebrows as the minister read over Dad's naval record, Battle Stars, medals, and certificates:

- 2 Battle stars for service on the USS *Vincennes* (CA-44)
- 14 Battle stars for service on the USS *Santa Fe* (CL-60)
- Commendation Medal
- Good Conduct Medal
- WWII Victory Medal
- American Defense Service Medal
- American Campaign Medal
- Asiatic Pacific Campaign Medal
- Navy Occupation Service Medal
- Navy Unit Commendation Ribbon
- Task Force 16 Commemorative Certificate – Doolittle Raid – California
- Navy Citation – Certificate of Participation–Doolittle Raid–Washington DC
- Bronze Star for Heroic Efforts in the Battle of Iwo Jima
- Philippine Liberation Ribbon
- Philippine Presidential Unit Citation

- "Order of the Ditch" (for passing through Panama Canal)
- "Order of the Shellback" (Certificate of Crossing – Equator)
- "Golden Shellback" (Certificate of Crossing – International Date Line)
- "Special Emerald Shellback" (Certificate of Crossing at the Greenwich Meridian)
- "Blue Nose" Certificate (Certificate of Crossing Arctic Circle)

When the service concluded, one of the sailors asked if I had been born "before or after" my father entered the Navy. I replied, "After." We both knew it was rather remarkable that E. J. Ridgeway had lived through his war experience to raise a family. He had not been just a seaman during the war, he was a fighting naval stalwart.

E. J. Ridgeway's war tale is told as a yeoman's story, without a great deal of fanfare drawn to his person, but with an emphasis on the adventure he encountered. A fantastic journey through the seas of the world at war, this book chronicles an entirely improbable warrior sailor. E. J. was not born into a militaristic family—his ancestors had fought only when necessary, yet with as much honor as possible for such an undesirable task.

Born as a man out of due time to a world that became as foreign to him as the ports he occupied, my father would return home without the language or tattoos often ascribed to sailors. An honorable man who I never heard curse, his story will be told so that it can be read by those he influenced in the spirit of those who influenced him.

He spoke very little of his war years, believing it was not to be told in front of women and children.

His account, as I discovered it, will take the reader behind the political maneuverings before and during World War II, and then on a journey across and through the Atlantic, Arctic, Caribbean, Pacific (north, central, and south), south China Sea, Indian Ocean, and the Sea of Japan, all the while watching a Seaman First Class survive the sinking of his first ship to become a GM/1c, Gunner's Mate First Class.

While training for war, he passed through German U-boat infested Atlantic waters on a secret mission into the Indian Ocean; a mission not divulged to the public for over 50 years. Interrupted by the Japanese attack on Pearl Harbor, he was ordered to return to the United States, through the Panama Canal, to join the Doolittle Bomber Run, an almost suicidal, retaliatory attack on Tokyo just four months later. For the next three and one-half years, my father fought the Japanese on two warships, on a journey, that could be compared to a 101 Introductory Course for World War II in the Pacific.

E. J. Ridgeway served before, during, and after the war on two cruisers, USS *Vincennes* (CA-44) and USS *Santa Fe* (CL-60), encompassing his enlistment period from November 1940 through October 1946. For family members who had ancestors serving on these two gallant ships during this time, I especially hope this book will provide valuable insight into the sacrifices made by their crew members who faithfully served their country during America's war in the Pacific.

USS VINCENNES – CA-44

Laid down: January 2, 1934 at Quincy, Massachusetts

Launched: May 21, 1936, sponsored by Miss Harriett Virginia Kimmell, daughter of Joseph Kimmell, Mayor of *Vincennes*, Indiana

Commissioned: February 24, 1937, Captain Burton H. Green in command

Dimensions: 588 feet long and 61 feet wide

Top Speed: 32 knots

Armaments: nine 8-inch, eight 5-inch, eight .50 caliber machine guns, and two 3-pounders, carrying four seaplanes

Class: The New Orleans class cruisers were a class of seven heavy cruisers built for the United States Navy in the 1930s. These ships participated in heavy surface battles during the Pacific War. The heavy cruiser was built for long range and high speed, to act as a fast scout and protective screen for a battle fleet with design parameters dictated by the Washington Naval Treaty of 1922 and the London Naval Treaty of 1930.

USS *Vincennes* (CA-44) was the second ship to bear the name.

Awarded Two Battle stars: Battle of Midway and Battle of Guadalcanal/Savo Island

USS *Vincennes* was sunk August 9, 1942 at the Battle of Savo Island, Guadalcanal

USS SANTA FE – CL-60

Laid down: June 7, 1941

Launched: June 10, 1942, sponsored by Miss Caroline T. Chavez

Commissioned: November 24, 1942, Captain Russell S. Berkey in command

Dimensions: 610 feet 1inch long and 66 feet 4 inches wide

Top Speed: 31.6 knots

Armaments: Twelve 6-inch .47 caliber guns, twelve 5-inch .38 caliber dual purpose plus 40 mm and 20 mm anti-aircraft guns

Class: Cleveland Class light cruiser was designed by the U.S. Navy specifically for World War II with increased cruising range, anti-aircraft armament, and torpedo protection. These cruisers served mainly in the Pacific Fleet during WWII, especially in the Fast Carrier Task Force.

USS *Santa Fe* (CL-60) was the first ship of the U.S. Navy to be named after the City of Santa Fe, New Mexico

Awarded 14 Battle stars: Aleutian Campaign, Pacific Raids, Bougainville Operation, Gilbert Islands Operation (Tarawa), Marshall Islands Operation, Asiatic-Pacific Raids, Western New Guinea Operations, Marianas Operation, Western Caroline Islands Operations, Philippine Liberation, Leyte Operation, Third Fleet Support Operations, Iwo Jima Operation, Okinawa Operation

E. J. RIDGEWAY'S JOURNEYS AND BATTLES

On the USS *VINCENNES* (CA-44):

- January/February 1941: Neutrality Patrols of America's recently acquired British Caribbean bases.

- March 1941: Equator Crossing. Ridgeway becomes a "Shellback."

- March 1941: "Gold Run." From Pernambuco, Brazil, the *Vincennes* is sent to Simon's Town, South Africa to transport a large shipment of British gold bullion to New York as payment for U.S. munitions, food, etc. per the Lend Lease Act.

- June - July 1941: Neutrality Patrols of Caribbean bases.

- August - September 1941: Escort for two convoy trips to Iceland carrying munitions and supplies.

- September 24, 1941: Arctic Crossing – Ridgeway receives "Blue Nose" Certificate.

- November - December 1941: "Secret" William Sail 12X Convoy. U.S. ships, including the *Vincennes*, escorted American transports carrying British troops destined for Singapore to Cape Town, South Africa.

- April 1942: Jimmy Doolittle Bomber Raid. USS *Vincennes* was part of the escort fleet for the carriers USS *Hornet* and *Enterprise*

- May 1942: Coral Sea Battle (*Vincennes* arrived the last day of battle)

- June 1942: Midway (*Vincennes* and Ridgeway's first Battle Star)

- August 7-9, 1942: Guadalcanal and Savo Island – (*Vincennes* and Ridgeway's second Battle Star). USS *Vincennes*, along with the USS *Quincy*, USS *Astoria*, and HMAS *Canberra* were sunk on August 9, 1942.
Ridgeway sustained a leg injury and concussion.

- September 1942: Treasure Island Naval Base. Ridgeway was detained on this base after the USS *Vincennes* sank and prior to his reassignment to the USS *Santa Fe*.

On the USS *SANTA FE* (CL-60): Assigned to ship in October 1942

- April 26-August 15, 1943: Aleutian Campaign: Attu Bombardment and Invasion, Kiska Bombardments (2) and Invasion. This was USS *Santa Fe's* first Battle Star and Ridgeway's third Battle Star.

- September – October 1943: Pacific Raids. Tarawa Strike and Wake Bombardment September 18 and October 5-6, 1943. USS *Santa Fe's* second Battle Star and Ridgeway's fourth Battle Star.

- November 8-9, 1943: Treasury-Bougainville Operation: Night Air Attack at Solomon Islands. USS *Santa Fe's* third Battle Star and Ridgeway's fifth Battle Star.

- November 20-22, 1943: Gilbert Islands Operation: Tarawa Invasion. USS *Santa Fe's* fourth Battle Star and Ridgeway's sixth Battle Star.

- December 4, 1943–February 2, 1944: Marshall Islands Operation: Kwajalein Air Strike, Wotje Bombardment, Kwajalein Invasion - *Santa Fe's* fifth Battle Star and Ridgeway's seventh Battle Star.

- February 16 - May 1, 1944: Asiatic-Pacific Raids: Truk, Saipan, Emirau, Palau, Yap, Truk & Ponape Strikes. USS *Santa Fe's* sixth Battle Star and Ridgeway's eighth Battle Star.

- April 21-22, 1944: Western New Guinea Operations: Hollandia Invasion and Wadke/Sawar Bombardment. USS *Santa Fe's* seventh Battle Star and Ridgeway's ninth Battle Star.

- June 11– August 5, 1944: Marianas Operation: Saipan Invasion, First Battle of the Philippine Sea "Turkey Shoot," Pagan Air Strike, Iwo Jima. Bombardment, Guam Invasion, Yap, Palau and Woleai Air Strikes, Bonins Surface Action, Chichi Jima Bombardment. USS *Santa Fe's* eighth Battle Star and Ridgeway's tenth Battle Star.

- September 6–24, 1944: Western Caroline Islands Operations - Palau Invasion, Mindanao Bislig Bay Action, East Leyte Air Strike, Manila/Luzon Air Strike, East Samar Air Strike

- September 16-18, 1944: In between actions, *Santa Fe* provided support for the Marine Landings on Peleliu Island (the "Forgotten Battle"). USS *Santa Fe's* ninth Battle Star and Ridgeway's 11th Battle Star.

- October 10-20, 1944: Philippine Liberation - Okinawa Air Strike, Formosa Air strike/Halsey's Bait Force, and Visayan Invasion. USS *Santa Fe's* tenth Battle Star and Ridgeway's 12th Battle Star.

- October 24–December 14-16, 1944: Leyte Operation (Originally known as Second Battle of the Philippine Sea) - Battle for Leyte Gulf Surface Action, East Leyte Air Strikes, Luzon Air Strike, Luzon (3 Air strikes). USS *Santa Fe's* 11th Battle Star and Ridgeway's 13th Battle Star.

- January 3–22, 1945: Third Fleet Supporting Operations: Formosa Air strikes (2), Luzon Air Strike, Camranh Bay, Indo-China Air Strike, Amroy, Hong Kong, China Air Strike, Formosa-Okinawa Air Strike. USS *Santa Fe's* 12th Battle Star and Ridgeway's 14th Battle Star.

- February 16-26, 1945: Iwo Jima Operation: Tokyo, Honshu Air strikes (2), Iwo Jima Invasion. USS *Santa Fe's* 13th Battle Star and Ridgeway's 15th Battle Star.

- March 18–23, 1945: Okinawa Operation: Kyushu, Shikoku USS *Franklin* Rescue. USS *Santa Fe's* 14th Battle Star /Ridgeway's 16th Battle Star.

- April 10-July 26, 1945: Stateside at Navy Yard.

- September 1–November 14, 1945: Occupation of Japan: Sasebo Occupation, Nagasaki Inspection, Wakayama Inspection, Tokyo Inspection, Ominato Occupation, Otaru Occupation, Hokodate Occupation, Aomori Occupation.

- Magic Carpet Ride - After Japan surrendered, the USS *Santa Fe* (CL-60) assisted in the Magic Carpet Ride—the transport of various American military troops back to the United States.

Introduction

1940 – A Pivotal Year

1940 was a year of change for E. J. Ridgeway. The year started with a bang, when General Neyland brought his undefeated Tennessee Volunteers to play Southern California on New Year's Day in the 26th Annual Rose Bowl game. A native southerner, E. J. was the only one among the boys from Dos Palos High School to cheer on the Volunteers. Tennessee entered the game as a favorite after shutting out all their opponents, but USC ended their winning streak as the Trojans scored the first points against the Volunteers all season. It was a shut-out victory of 14-0 and a letdown for Ridgeway. However, his disappointment was quickly forgotten when he celebrated his 18th birthday nine days later.

1940 was also a year of change for the United States as conflict in countries to the east and west was on the rise. The United States and its allies had already begun political maneuverings to develop an unprepared U.S. military for possible combat against Hitler's invasion of Europe. On September 16, 1940, the Selective Training and Service Act was signed into law by President Roosevelt, creating the first peacetime draft in United States history. The Act required that all men between the ages of 21 and 35 register with local draft boards. With the rearming of U.S. forces, the Great Depression was finally beginning to ease, but soon Pearl Harbor would officially mark America's entrance into the Second World War.

At age six, Ellie Jay Ridgeway had lost his mother to tuberculosis, a death which left his father, Russell, a widower. Russell had five boys, ages 15 and younger, to raise by himself. This was quite a blow to the Ridgeway family, who, like so many under the gloom of the Great Depression, were already struggling for the everyday necessities of life. When the opportunity arose for 12-year old E. J. to live with his uncle in California, the young boy from Alabama was up for the challenge. Later, when he signed up for a six-year stint with the U.S. Navy in November of 1940, it was no surprise that Ridgeway was once again ready to travel to places unknown.

During basic training, Ridgeway's talent for handling and maintaining firearms eventually placed him at the gunner's helm. Life in Sand Mountain, Alabama had prepared him well. At an early age, Ridgeway learned the skills needed to keep his shotgun in working condition in order to shoot moving targets for food and tin cans for target practice.

His naval journeys would begin on the heavy cruiser USS *Vincennes* (CA-44). Naturally, Ridgeway was assigned to the ship's gunnery division for training on one of her five-inch guns.

PART I

USS *VINCENNES* – CA-44

THE "VINNIE MARU"

CHAPTER ONE

NEUTRALITY PATROLS AND GOLD RUNS

USS Vincennes (CA-44): Background

Laid down at the Fore River Shipyard in January 1934, USS *Vincennes* (CA-44) was the final member of the New Orleans Class of heavy cruisers that were built according to specifications of the Washington Naval Treaty of 1922. Originally classified as a light cruiser because of her thin armor, she was later reclassified as a heavy cruiser because of her eight-inch guns.

USS *Vincennes* lay anchored off Tompkinsville, New York, under the command of Captain John D. Beardall, on the day Hitler marched into Poland on September 1, 1939. Four days later, the United States Navy ordered air and surface patrols to observe and report movements of the warships of Axis nations in the Caribbean waters off the coasts of North and South America. *Vincennes* became part of the warships of the Atlantic Squadron Neutrality Patrol on September 14, 1939. Through the spring of 1940, the USS *Vincennes* began conducting Neutrality Patrols off Cape Hatteras, North Carolina then ranging into the Caribbean Sea and Gulf of Yucatan (Mexico).

First Gold Run

When Germany invaded and occupied Austria in 1938 and Czechoslovakia in 1939, Hitler seized the gold from the governments of both countries to fund his war machine. The Polish government, prior to the invasion of their country, sent most of their gold to France, but soon the French found themselves under Nazi threat. European countries about to come under Hitler's heel began shipping massive amounts of gold to the United States in the Spring of 1940.

On May 28, 1940, the U.S. Ambassador to France requested that President Roosevelt send American warships to deliver weapons to France and embark French and Belgian gold reserves for transport back to the United States for safekeeping. In response to the Ambassador's request, USS *Vincennes* secretly sortied from Hampton Roads, Virginia with destroyers USS *Truxton* and USS *Simpson* and arrived at Casablanca, French Morocco on June 9, 1940.

As the ships began loading the 200 tons of precious metal onto the *Vincennes,* they received word of Italy's declaration of war on Great Britain and France. The gold, estimated at a value of $490,000,000 (1940 U.S. dollars), was the largest amount yet to be shipped on a single vessel. The *Vincennes* arrived at New York City with the hoard of gold on June 20, 1940, which was quickly deposited into U.S. banks. Afterward, *Vincennes* resumed her routine patrols.

Ridgeway Assigned to USS *Vincennes*

Due to the Navy's urgent need for gunmen, after completion of his final week of basic training, E. J. Ridgeway was given an immediate ship assignment. In January 1941, when he first walked up the gangplank of the USS *Vincennes,* anchored at Hampton Roads, Virginia, Europe was at war and America was being drawn into it. The heavy cruiser would be Seaman Ridgeway's home for the next twenty months.

On the USS *Vincennes*, E. J. would learn to use the dual-purpose mounted 5"/38 caliber gun with AA shell fuse setters, designed to be effective against both surface and air targets. With an elevation of 85 degrees and power ramming, the five-inch gun was capable of rapid-firing at high angles against aircraft. The high rate of fire for this gun, with a well-trained crew, could be 22 rounds per minute per barrel for short periods of time. For the Pacific battles that lay ahead of the *Vincennes*, Ridgeway would get plenty of on-the-job training on this gun.

Seaman Ridgeway's first foreign port was Guantanamo Bay when the Vincennes arrived in Cuba January 1941, and took patrol of the neutral waters of the Caribbean. War was in the air, and the U.S. Navy had to prepare their sailors for the impending fight. During this time, the ship conducted battle practice and gunnery exercises in company with other warships. After a short patrol of the waters around

Jamaica, the ship headed for Puerto Rico and engaged in land exercises and fire support through the month of February.

Ridgeway Becomes a Shellback

Barely two months a sailor, Ridgeway was about to experience his first ritual at sea. After leaving Puerto Rico in March 1941, the shipmates of the *Vincennes* were told to "look for the bump in the ocean" as they were about to cross the equator and graduate from Polliwogs to Shellbacks. The two-day ceremonial crossing would begin with a Subpoena Summons from Neptunus Rex, Ruler of the Raging Main to all the "loathsome polliwogs, landlubbers, sea lawyers, floor-flushers" and various other crude names ascribed to all the uninitiated on the *Vincennes*.

The Official Greetings and Warnings and the orders for Neptune's Day were then read out. After the sailors' completed their daily routines, the announcement was made, "Break Neptune's Flag at Main!"

The Royal Party arrived at the forward part of the ship's upper deck to induct the slimy Polliwogs into the mysteries of the deep. After a full inspection of all divisions, "King Neptune" then took to his throne to observe the ceremonial hazing for all Polliwogs on board. Afterward, all of the initiates became trusted Shellbacks.

Second Gold Run

After crossing the equator, USS *Vincennes* made a temporary stop at Pernambuco, Brazil on March 17 en route to her ultimate destination at Simon's Town, South Africa for another gold run. There, the ship took on a large shipment of gold bullion to pay for arms purchased by Great Britain from the United States. The ship was on her way back by March 30. Dad said that upon their arrival in New York with the precious metal, all men departing the ship were first patted down to ensure there was no theft.

In April 1941, the *Vincennes* was in dry dock at Norfolk Naval Yard during which time, Captain Frederick Riefkohl replaced John Beardall as skipper. Riefkohl was a World War I veteran and recipient of the Navy Cross.

Vincennes returned to her patrol as part of Atlantic Neutrality Squadron, Patrol Task Group 1, in company with the carrier *Ranger* and destroyers *Sampson* and *Eberle* and set out from Bermuda to begin a 4,675-mile neutrality patrol of that area through May 23. During this time the Royal Navy sank the German battleship *Bismarck* in the North Atlantic near France, sparking more defensive action by the United States. President Roosevelt immediately declared an unlimited state of emergency, extended the boundaries of the Atlantic Neutrality Patrol, and transferred the Pacific Fleet units to the Atlantic. From May 31 – July 15, *Vincennes* conducted a 4,550-mile neutrality patrol from Bermuda to Hampton Roads, Virginia and then back to Bermuda.

Detached from the Atlantic Patrol Squadron, *Vincennes* left Bermuda headed for the States. By late July 1941, she was among a convoy of U.S. warships escorting transports loaded with war supplies and munitions destined for Iceland. Six destroyers encircled the steaming formation consisting of one battleship, four cruisers, and six cargo and transport ships. The choppy seas of the North Atlantic, with its colder temperatures and strong winds, were quite the contrast from the smooth, calm waters of the balmy Caribbean where *Vincennes* had been patrolling. The ships plowed through the Atlantic waters infested with German U-boats prowling through the dense fog.

Seaman Ridgeway had his first view of Iceland when the U.S. ships arrived off her coast on August 6, 1941. After the flight squadron took off from the carrier for the landing, the *Vincennes* and her fleet turned course back to Norfolk.

The return trip through the turbulent North Atlantic turned into a battle with the elements. The *Vincennes* was pounded by strong winds and heavy rains, and her inexperienced crew wondered if they would make it back alive. The weather cleared temporarily that night but a storm front moved in the next morning. For the next two days, all seamen second or third class, including Ridgeway, were forbidden above deck in the rough seas, and held onto whatever they could as the fierce winds and churning waves tossed their ship about. On August 14, *Vincennes* left the convoy, and the anxious sailors breathed a sigh of relief when they finally arrived at the States.

As the war intensified in Europe, the Atlantic waters became more and more threatening for American vessels. In preparation for her second voyage to Iceland, the *Vincennes* conducted intense shooting exercises through early September. A lighthearted aspect of the training was competition between the ships' gunners. Shore-based patrol boats pulled sleds with bulls-eye targets while the gunners took aim and kept score. Cheers from the gun mounts could be heard from the winning ship.

On September 4, 1941, the destroyer USS *Greer* was fired upon while tracking a German U-boat 175 miles southwest of Iceland, but no contact was made. In one of his "fireside chats" on September 11, President Roosevelt used this incident to garner support of the war in Europe. The United States Navy became more aggressive and issued orders to attack any vessel threatening American shipping or ships under U.S. escort.

While the news of the German attack on the USS *Greer* flashed across America on September 5, 1941, the *Vincennes* was once again part of a U.S. escort convoy. This convoy included a battleship, another cruiser, and four destroyers, carrying war munitions and supplies to Iceland. The battleship led the convoy while the cruisers moved alongside of the merchant ships, and the destroyers provided the screening for the entire fleet. En route, the ships sighted multiple German subs but no action was taken.

The U.S. fleet docked at Reykjavik, Iceland by mid-September 1941, and *Vincennes* was at port there for one month. On September 23, the *Vincennes* and an accompanying destroyer left the Reykjavik Harbor and sailed north crossing the Arctic Circle, a feat few surface ships had accomplished at that time. Ridgeway and his shipmates were now "Blue Noses."

During this time, the *Vincennes* patrolled back and forth between Iceland and Greenland, avoiding large chunks of floating ice, and then sighted her first iceberg. The ship sailed under the "Northern Lights." These polar lights, also known as the Aurora Borealis,

27

displayed amazing color formations in the Arctic sky, where night can be as long as six months. The *Vincennes* left her North Atlantic patrol and anchored at Newfoundland on October 11, 1941.

While the *Vincennes* and her convoy encountered no German threats during their Icelandic voyage, several days later, on October 17, 1941, the destroyer USS *Kearny* was torpedoed and damaged southwest of Iceland.

Upon arrival at the Charleston Navy Yard in Boston, the crew received news that the destroyer USS *Reuben James,* which had sailed in both their convoys to Iceland, had been torpedoed and sunk by a German submarine while escorting a convoy of merchant ships bound for Great Britain. By late autumn of 1941, American naval forces in the Atlantic found themselves in a de facto war with Germany. On November 6, 1941, the cruiser USS *Omaha* and the destroyer USS *Somers* captured the German blockade runner *Odenwald* disguised as a U.S. ship, the *Willmoto.*

During this time, USS *Vincennes* was about to be assigned another mission to South African waters. This was a top secret mission that had been conceived after the August 1941 Atlantic Charter Conference between President Roosevelt and England's Prime Minister Winston Churchill. The two leaders set in motion a plan to transport British troops to the Middle East aboard six U.S. transports, three of which were former luxury liners. To skirt the boundaries of the 1939 Neutrality Act, Roosevelt proposed a route via Halifax, Nova Scotia, instead of the United States. Seven weeks before America officially entered World War II, the United States Navy received orders to participate in this clandestine voyage that would eventually span nearly the entire globe.

On October 20, 1941, the captains of eighteen U.S. Navy warships and transports moored at four East Coast naval bases, received a six-page OpNav message stamped "SECRET" from Admiral H. R. Stark, Chief of Naval Operations. The message contained details for the detachment of a United States convoy of warships, designated Task Force 14, to transport 20,000 British troops to the Middle East via Halifax. The end of the message, copied to the Commander-in-Chief of the Atlantic Fleet, along with four other Navy Commands, stressed the "highly secretive nature of the movements and plans of this expedition" and emphasized non-disclosure to anyone outside of those immediately involved.

The least known in U.S. Navy annals, U.S. Task Force 14 would remain hidden from public record for over four decades after the war. E. J. Ridgeway and the crew of the *Vincennes* would be among the American warships of Task Force 14, escorting the William Sail 12X Convoy carrying British troops to their eventual doom. It would also be the *Vincennes'* last pre-war journey.

CHAPTER TWO

U.S. TASK FORCE 14 AND THE WILLIAM SAIL 12X

CONVOY

On a gray, indistinct morning, October 28, 1941, at 7:00 a.m., the William Sail 12X Convoy—dubbed "Winston's Special" by the men on the ships—left Liverpool, England for Halifax, Nova Scotia, destined for the Middle East. Aboard the eight vintage transports (seven British and one Polish) were approximately 20,000 British officers and men of the 18th Volunteer Infantry Division. They had boarded at the Princess Jetty, part of the large Princess Landing Stage on the Mersey River.

After the British transports left the huge dock, they merged at the mouth of the Clyde River in Scotland with HMS *Exeter*, HMS *Dorsetshire*, and four destroyers as escorts. It was a time in the war when German raiders and U-boats roamed the Atlantic at will, making the waters treacherous while America was still abiding by the Neutrality Act of 1939—or so it appeared.

News of the sinking of the USS *Reuben James* was not received by the WS 12X Convoy until October 31, 1941. The destroyer was the first American warship to be sunk by one of Hitler's submarines. In response to this attack, President Roosevelt ordered all American warships in the Atlantic, including those escorting the WS 12X Convoy, to fire on any enemy submarines sighted in the waters.

It was quite a relief, as well as a morale boost, when the clandestine British convoy first sighted their American escorts. On November 2, 1941, the Adjutant of the First Cambridgeshire Regiment of the 18th Division recorded, "At 0830, the mast of a fleet was seen over the horizon on the starboard side. A most impressive sight." Two planes flew over the convoy from USS *Yorktown*, and Task Force 14.3, which included the USS *New Mexico*, an oil tanker, and Destroyer Squadron 2. The light cruisers, USS *Philadelphia* and USS *Savannah* also joined in the formation.

The morning of November 5, 1941, the six American transport ships began arriving in Halifax from four different U.S. ports. USS *West Point* (former luxury liner SS *America*), USS *Mount Vernon* (former luxury liner SS *Washington*), USS *Wakefield* (former luxury liner SS *Manhattan*), USS *Orizaba*, USS *Joseph T. Dickman* and USS *Leonard Wood* would carry the British troops of the 18th Division to their destination.

Captain D. B. Beary on the USS *Mount Vernon* was the convoy commander. Task Force 14's Commodore was Rear Admiral Arthur B.

Cook, Commander Air Force Atlantic Fleet, who flew his flag from the carrier USS *Ranger.*

After a few close calls due to poor visibility and a phantom U-boat scare, all six transports were supplied and waiting to load the English troops, who had crept into the foggy Halifax Harbor the morning of November 6. By the evening of November 9, all troops destined for the Middle East were aboard the six American transport ships.

The *Vincennes* left Portland, Maine, November 10, 1941, steaming north to Canada, about ten miles from Halifax. Task Force 14 now consisted of the USS *Ranger* CV-4 (carrier), USS *Vincennes* CA-44 (heavy cruiser), USS *Quincy* CA-39 (heavy cruiser), and eight destroyers: USS *Wainwright,* USS *Mayrant,* USS *Trippe,* USS *Rhind,* USS *Winslow,* USS *McDougal,* USS *Rowan,* and USS *Moffet.* A Canadian destroyer, HMCS *Annapolis,* provided a brief shield for the American ships while destroyers searched the Atlantic for German submarines. USS *Vincennes,* with Task Force 14, joined the American transports, loaded with 20,000 British soldiers, and headed out for the open seas as escorts for the William Sail 12X Convoy.

Scout planes from the carrier *Ranger* were augmented by the float planes from the *Vincennes* and *Quincy* to assist in screening for enemy subs during the voyage. Rumor among the crew was that the carrier and eight destroyers were to be left behind when they arrived at Trinidad, and then the cruisers would head for Cape Town with the transports.

At midnight, November 12, 1941, the *Vincennes* temporarily detached from the convoy to allow the ship's surgeon to perform an

33

emergency appendectomy on one of the crewman. E. J. Ridgeway mentioned that he had such a surgery while on the *Vincennes*. I can only assume that my father may have been the sailor being "stitched up" in this report.

As the convoy approached Port of Spain, ten patrol planes out of Borinquen Field, Puerto Rico, joined the U.S. convoy, providing them with anti-submarine surveillance. The following day, November 16, 1941, the land-based planes flew to Trinidad providing the convoy maximum air cover during their most vulnerable time as they entered the harbor.

By now, oil tanker *Cimarron* had joined the convoy. All U.S. ships were anchored at Trinidad, Port of Spain, on November 17. The vessels replenished the next day, and on November 19 left Trinidad for the 6,000-mile South Atlantic crossing to Cape Town—the longest leg of the voyage.

The three converted luxury liners among the U.S. transport ships had been fitted with World War I weapons, but their accuracy against moving targets was questionable. Evasive action was their best defense. To avoid enemy submarines, the convoy sailed in a zigzag pattern during daylight hours and at night, it was "lights out" from sunset to sunrise. All hands were at General Quarters during the blackout. There was more than one enemy sub reportedly sighted, but no contact was made.

Seaman Ridgeway had already entered the Shellback brotherhood when the *Vincennes* passed over the equator during their gold run to Cape Town in March of 1941. However, many of the navy men were still Pollywogs and unprepared for what lay ahead for them as they approached Neptune's Domain the day after Thanksgiving, on November 21. The ritual hazing involved the drinking of obnoxious concoctions, head-shavings, and a run through a slop line of Thanksgiving left-overs. The ceremony ended with each Pollywog yelling out, "Shellback!" Then, it was back to business at hand—the transport of 20,000 British soldiers to the Middle East.

On Wednesday, November 26, the convoy moved slowly as the *Cimarron* refueled the transports. On Thursday, the *Leonard Wood* reported a submarine surface, but no action was taken. The carrier *Ranger*, and destroyers *Rhind* and *Trippe* detached from the convoy and headed back to Trinidad. Air cover was now dependent upon the heavy cruisers *Vincennes* and *Quincy* as their "gooney bird" planes began their rotation.

On November 30, 1941, HMS *Dorsetshire* of the Royal Navy reported she had downed the *Python*, a German supply ship 860 miles to the southeast of the convoy. *Dorsetshire* trained all her guns broadside and opened fire. The Python went to the bottom—stern first—and the enemy U-boats remained in the area to rescue her survivors. Had the *Dorsetshire* not sunk the *Python*, the German U-boats would have been refueled, resupplied, and waiting to attack the WS 12X Convoy at their most vulnerable time as they entered the port of Cape Town.

British Navy discovers German "Ultra" and "Enigma"

The detection of the *Python's* location by the British had not been mere chance. Winston Churchill and his intelligence staff had a

35

secret weapon hidden in their pocket. Earlier, in May of 1941, the Royal Navy had captured the ultra-secret German deciphering machines used to vector the enemy U-boats to Allied convoys and instruct Nazi supply ships. With "Ultra" and "Enigma" in British hands, the Royal Navy had guided the American warships and the WS 12X Convoy safely to all ports. It was a fact unknown to the convoy and even the President of the United States at that time—another secret of World War II that would not be made public for the next three decades.

By December 6, Task Force 14 and the William Sail 12X Convoy were south of Cape of Good Hope. The winds shifted and the seas became increasingly rough as the South Atlantic collided with the Indian Ocean. The *Vincennes* sighted a Japanese freighter riding low in the waters. It appeared to be loaded with steel and headed for Japan. Dad said the *Vincennes* had her guns trained on the suspicious vessel, but the order to fire was never given.

On December 7, 1941, WS 12X Convoy entered the "Roaring Forties" (the strong westerly winds of the Southern Hemisphere), and the upheaval broke the securing lines of one of the float planes on the *Vincennes*. It was lost overboard. The last report that evening stated that "the seas are quite rough." However, the situation was about to get rougher. Two hours later, the convoy was radioed:

"Japan has bombed Pearl Harbor!"

CHAPTER THREE

AMERICA DECLARES WAR

William Sail 12X Convoy Reroutes to Singapore

When Task Force 14 received news of the Pearl Harbor attack, Convoy WS 12X had passed the Cape of Agulhas (the geographic southern tip of the African Continent) headed for Durbin on the east coast of South Africa. With America now at war on both sides of her continent, the convoy and her U.S. escorts changed course and hurried back to Cape Town. The cruisers, transports and *Cimarron* anchored in the harbor while the destroyers guarded the entrance. Their final destination was now in question as Roosevelt and Churchill mulled over the consequences of Japan's "act of infamy."

For Churchill, the Japanese threat to the colonial British Empire in the East Indies was immediate. Vital materials from her colonies were crucial to the survival of the United Kingdom. The Prime Minister decided that the 18th Division onboard the William Sail 12X Convoy would proceed to Singapore via Bombay, India, to shore up Lt. General Arthur Percival's 65,000 men in defense of their 100-million-dollar naval base.

While America was reeling from the surprise attack on Pearl Harbor, Japan was approaching Britain's "impregnable fortress" at Singapore from all directions. On December 10, 1941, British warships HMS *Repulse* and HMS *Prince of Wales,* without air support, were targeted off the coast of Malaya and sunk by Japanese war planes. Admiral Sir Dudley Pound phoned Churchill of the disaster. The Prime Minister recounted this moment in his memoirs, "In all the war I never received a more direct shock." He realized there were no British or American capital ships in the Indian Ocean or Pacific. He later wrote, "Over all this vast expanse of waters Japan was supreme, and we everywhere were weak and naked."

The fate of the 20,000 British soldiers of the 18th Division would be decided only a few days after their arrival at Singapore, which was being hit hard by the Japanese from the air, the sea, and by land. Quickly consolidated into the British forces, including Indian and Australian troops fighting on the island, the 18th Division was among the 85,000 troops surrendered by Lt. General Percival on February 15, 1942, to the Japanese Lt. General Tomoyuki Yamashita. Most of these prisoners of war would end up in Burma and Thailand to build the infamous "Death Railway."

E. J. Ridgeway grieved out loud several times after the war, thinking his ship had helped take "those British Boys" to the Bataan Death March. He was mistaken as to their destination—but the result was just as horrible.

The *Vincennes, Quincy,* and *Cimarron* anchored in Cape Town Harbor on December 9, 1941. While the cruisers remained in the harbor, the destroyers served as escort for the WS 12X Convoy for one more day until they were relieved by a British heavy cruiser. Detached from the convoy, the U.S. destroyers rejoined the awaiting warships for return to the States. On December 16, the crew of the *Vincennes*, in company with the *Quincy, Cimarron* and six destroyers, took a last glance at Cape Town unsure of their next destination.

Everyone looked forward to a peaceful Christmas, but knew that could change if contact was made with the enemy. On Saturday, December 20, there was still no war news. The sailors were jittery and anxious for any information that would indicate America's plans to avenge Pearl Harbor. The day before, the crew was informed that the only orders for the *Vincennes* were to escort the *Cimarron* back to the States.

On the morning of December 21, 1941, Major-General Merton Beckwith-Smith, Commander of the 18th (East Anglican) Division sent a message thanking the crews of the Quincy, Vincennes, and the destroyers for their protection of the British Army troops.

First Christmas on the Vincennes: December 25, 1941

The convoy was on course north of Brazil, and Christmas morning, Chaplain Schwyhart conducted a special church service.

39

Afterward, a holiday meal was served, and the crew was treated to a movie that afternoon. For many of the sailors, it would be their first time away from home during the holiday season.

Christmas had always been a reminder of his mother's death for E. J. Ridgeway. The seventh of nine children born to Russell and Georgia Ridgeway, he was profoundly influenced throughout his young life by his mother's devotion to God. Georgia lost her battle with tuberculosis on December 23, 1929. Because of the fear of spreading the contagious disease, a hasty burial was required the next day. The snow-covered ground on the 24th had melted to slush, which in turn became deep mud that made the road to the grave by wagon impassable. On Christmas day, a team of four horses finally made the trip to Wynnville Cemetery. The seven-year-old E. J. held tightly to his Christmas presents—an apple, an orange, and a red rubber ball— as his mother was laid to rest. No doubt, these would have been the memories running through my father's mind as he experienced his first Christmas on the *Vincennes*.

Upon arrival in Norfolk early January 1942, *Vincennes* moved on to New York to begin the process of radar installation. By the end of the month, she left for Key West to escort the new ships USS *Hornet* (CV-8), USS *North Carolina* (BB-55), and USS *Washington* (BB-56) on their maiden voyage. The *North Carolina* and the *Washington* were part of a new line of North Carolina-class battleships. They were faster and more fuel efficient and carried nine 16-inch and 20 five-inch cannons.

For Ridgeway, practicing on his five-inch gun was an almost daily occurrence. He became adept at all phases of the gun, from the sending up of the powder cases and projectiles from the magazines below, to the practice of loading and firing the cannon itself. Though the *Vincennes* had nine 8-inch guns, no one yet realized that the multi-purpose, anti-aircraft five-inch cannon would become one of the most important weapons on the sea.

Through the month of February, *Vincennes* continued her refitting for future combat. In early March 1942, she left Boston Harbor to engage in another top secret mission—her first operation of the war.

42

CHAPTER FOUR

AMERICA PREPARES TO STRIKE BACK

The surprise attack on Pearl Harbor was an overwhelming victory for the Japanese that severely crippled the United States Pacific Fleet. The Empire of the Rising Sun was a fast moving military machine that had already been proven in China, then had struck the Philippines, before moving through Burma and the Celebes. Malaya was being invaded for her raw materials and used as a backdoor for the attack on Singapore. Admiral Isoroku Yamamoto was truly "running wild in the Pacific."

Despite the shocking results of the Japanese attack, there was still hope. Three American aircraft carriers had been in the Pacific—none had been in port at Pearl Harbor on December 7. The USS *Lexington* (CV-2) was at Midway Island, the USS *Saratoga* (CV-3) was patrolling the west coast of the United States, and the USS *Enterprise* (CV-6) was at Wake Island.

The U.S. military began immediate plans for a counterattack. On January 10, 1942—Seaman Ridgeway's 20th birthday—the newly appointed Admiral Ernest J. King, Chief of U.S. Naval Operations, and Captain Francis Low, U.S. Submarine Commander, initiated a series of meetings to develop an epiphany. Low had received this insight at Norfolk, while observing planes practicing short distance takeoffs on the outline of a carrier deck painted on the ground. Low's idea to fly bombers off of a carrier deck to attack Tokyo from the air grew into a top secret mission coordinated by Captain Low, Captain Donald "Wu" Duncan (Admiral King's Air Operations Officer), and eventually, Lieutenant James "Jimmy" Doolittle. B-25 Mitchell bombers performed a trial run from the new carrier, USS *Hornet*. By February 1, 1942, the top-secret mission was in motion, with Jimmy Doolittle in charge.

Lieutenant Doolittle was provided with intelligence reports, complete with maps and charts of the targeted cities of Tokyo, Yokohama, Nagoya, Kobe, and Osaka. These included positions of naval targets, refineries, and military and industrial complexes. After bombing these targets, the planes would land at Chuchow, China for refueling with a final destination—Chungking. The first plane would carry four incendiary bombs that would light the way for the following planes, each carrying one incendiary and three demolition bombs.

Over twenty B-25 Mitchell bombers were modified for the mission. Since the planes would be flying as close to the water as possible, the lower ventral turrets were removed, reducing the weight of each plane by over 500 pounds. The fuel load was increased by installing 40-gallon gas tanks where the turret had been. The wings were lined with rubberized gas tanks. Gun placement was completed and the tail of each bomber was now "guarded" by two, black-painted broomsticks as dummy guns. The top-secret Norden bomb sight, useless for low altitude, was replaced with a make-shift aluminum sight, dubbed the "Mark Twain." These new bomb sights cost a grand total of 20 cents each and had been designed by Captain Charles "Ross" Greening.

Doolittle worked feverishly, sorting out problems and coordinating the training of the carefully selected pilots at Eglin Air Force Base in Pensacola, Florida. Doolittle also had a secret of his own. He planned to fly the first B-25 off the deck of the carrier *Hornet* when the raiders headed for Japan.

Early in March 1942, the *Vincennes* and light cruiser *Nashville*, steaming from Boston, picked up four destroyers and a tanker at New York Harbor. Off the Virginia Capes, the fleet was joined by the aircraft carrier *Hornet,* under the command of Captain Marc A. Mitscher. The ships next proceeded southward, passing between Cuba and Haiti and arriving at the Panama Canal on March 11, 1942.

Passage through the locks of the canal, where the Atlantic runs into the Pacific, was like going up and down a flight of stairs. When the hours-long ordeal was finished, Seaman Ridgeway would receive the "Order of the Ditch" certificate. *Vincennes* and the *Hornet* fleet arrived at San Diego, California on March 20. A day later, the ships steamed up the West Coast to San Francisco and entered Mare Island Naval Base.

While the *Hornet* and *Vincennes* were passing through the canal zone, "Wu" Duncan met with Admiral Chester Nimitz in Honolulu and arranged for a 16-ship task force to meet at a predetermined coordinate west of Hawaii. Duncan alerted General "Hap" Arnold that the Navy was in place. During the third week in March, he wired Admiral King, "Tell Jimmy to get on his horse." It was time to move forward with this mission.

On the morning of March 23, 1942, Doolittle called his crews together and gave them a last warning about the secrecy of the mission and stressed that they not divulge information to another soul.

Captain Edward "Ski" York was at Alameda Naval Air Station in California with Doolittle as the bombers landed from Eglin. Each pilot was asked if his "ship" performed properly. If the airman answered in the negative, the plane was parked at a nearby hangar. When all had landed and passed York and Doolittle's inspection, sixteen B-25s were deemed suitable. Doolittle instructed York to have the planes and all air crews board the *Hornet* while he met with Admiral William "Bull" Halsey, Captain Miles Browning (Halsey's Chief-of-Staff), and Donald "Wu" Duncan at the Fairmont Hotel in San Francisco.

Duncan laid out the fleet arrangement. Captain Mitscher of the *Hornet*, with the B-25s aboard, would be supported by the heavy cruiser *Vincennes*, light cruiser *Nashville*, destroyers *Gwin*, *Meredith*, *Monssen,* and *Grayson*, and the tanker *Cimarron*, designated Task

Force 16.2. Admiral Halsey on the *Enterprise* would be escorted by the heavy cruisers *Northampton* and *Salt Lake City*, destroyers *Fanning, Ellet, Balch,* and *Benham*, and tanker *Sabine* as Task Force 16.1.

The fleet was to rendezvous at a predetermined coordinate west of Hawaii on Sunday, April 12, and refuel from the tankers 800 miles off the coast of Japan. The destroyers and tankers would detach themselves there, and the remaining ships, *Hornet, Vincennes, Nashville, Enterprise, Salt Lake City,* and *Northampton* would finish their role in the mission. Before the officers left the table, they had agreed for the escorts to take the raiders as close as 400 miles from the Japanese mainland, if conditions permitted.

Japanese Admiral Chuichi Nagumo had devastated the Allied fleet in the East Indies, so the Navy's concern was for its Pacific carriers and the possible danger to the fleet posed by Japanese submarines. Four battleships had been sunk and four more damaged at Pearl Harbor, along with damage to three of the eight cruisers. With Nagumo's current location undetermined, the United States could not afford to forfeit any more capital ships. Protection of the carrier *Hornet* would be paramount in this mission.

When the sixteenth and last B-25 was hoisted aboard the *Hornet* and tied down in the early morning darkness of April 1, 1942, the carrier, along with her escorts, moved out into San Francisco Bay. The ships anchored at Berth 9, ready to set sail the next day. With Jimmy Doolittle aboard, the scuttlebutt was that rather than being transported and flown to an island base, an attack must be in the works. Where? No one had a clue.

As the *Vincennes* lay in anchor at San Francisco Bay, Seaman E. J. Ridgeway was on watch at his five-inch gun. Nearby was the naval base on Treasure Island, the former home of the Golden Gate Exposition (which eventually became known as "The San Francisco 1939 World's Fair"). Only 18 months prior, in September 1940, Ridgeway had attended that fair when the island was a grandiose "Magic City" of lights. The theme of the fair was physically symbolized by "The Tower of the Sun" along with a giant, 80-foot statue of Pacifica, goddess of the Pacific Ocean.

While Europe was already at war, "Pacifica" herself was not yet in the conflict. One of the major attractions was the "Port of the Trade Winds," featuring the China Clipper—the name-sake of Pan Am's famous fleet of long-range, trans-Pacific flying boats—which unwittingly gave the Japanese visitors a first-hand look at America's other openly displayed planes, military ships, and weapons.

Ultimately, the San Francisco Fair/Golden Gate Exposition failed to achieve its economic and political goals with neighboring countries in the Pacific. According to Richard Miller (a.k.a. Sparkletack):

> *"On September 29, 1940, the lights of the Golden Gate*
> *International Exposition went out forever. As the*
> *merchants and exhibitors packed their bags and glumly*
> *counted their receipts, Nazi Germany had begun a*
> *terror bombing campaign from the skies above London.*
> *And across the Pacific, Imperial Japan was planning a*

surprise attack on a United States naval base in Hawaii,
turning the concept of "Pacific Unity" into a hollow
joke."

In 1941, just prior to war being declared on Japan, the United States Navy seized Treasure Island for use as a naval base. The statue of Pacifica was immediately toppled to the ground, and all displays and theme parks from the World's Fair were demolished. The only remnants left standing were the administration building and hangars, now utilized by the Navy.

As the *Vincennes* crew prepared to steam into the Pacific the next day, Seaman Ridgeway had no way of knowing he would be back on Treasure Island in less than six months, almost two years to the date of his first visit. Only this time, he and hundreds of other sailors would be detained on the island under U.S. Marine guard.

On April 2, 1942, the U.S. warships pulled anchor, one by one, from San Francisco as heavy fog hung over the bay, slashing visibility to less than 1,000 yards. The light cruiser *Nashville* was underway around 7:45 a.m. accompanied by the destroyers *Gwin, Grayson, Monssen,* and *Meredith.* The *Hornet,* with Doolittle and his army officers and enlisted men onboard, left three hours later, followed by the *Vincennes* and the *Cimarron.* With sailors manning the rails, the ships steamed under the San Francisco Bay Bridge sliding past Alcatraz Island, and then under the Golden Gate Bridge into the Pacific.

Heading west, the *Hornet* and her escort conducted days of gunnery and damage control drills, anti-aircraft practice, and even night gunnery drills. During this time, there was concern as to the *Hornet's* preparedness for effective action in the possible event of an attack. Her crowded flight deck made it impossible for her own planes to take off should the need arise.

The word "Japan" was mentioned officially for the first time the next morning, April 3, 1942. Doolittle called the pilots together in the mess hall and proceeded to tell them they were going straight to Japan to bomb Tokyo and other targeted cities. Doolittle told the men it would take some time to get to the launch point, and there was still much work to be done. He again gave all the opportunity to change their mind as there were back-up pilots aboard. None did.

Navy PBY Catalina seaplanes escorted the task force until late that afternoon. The last contact was made by Navy Blimp L-8, delivering navigator domes. Afterward, all communications were carried out by semaphore flags. E. J. Ridgeway later recalled that as the domes were lowered onto the *Hornet,* the raid was announced. Spontaneous cheers from the men slowly quietened into silence, as the reality of their first engagement with the enemy set in. The yeoman of the ships talked among themselves about the "Jimmy Doolittle Bomber Run."

Doolittle's Army pilots adjusted to the Navy's protocol. They learned procedures for boarding a ship and "sea talk," but some things had to be experienced firsthand. When the B-25s were coming into San Francisco and the pilots observed the *Hornet* from the air, she looked small. As the airmen prepared to board and saw the carrier up close, they were in awe of her size.

The Navy boys got a kick out of helping the "lost" pilots below deck through the maze of hallways, hangars, engine room, plotting room, offices, sailors' quarters, and mess halls. Unprepared for the sailors' card and dice skills, the "fly boys" lost most of their paycheck to the seamen. Not all time was spent on gambling; there was still much preparation ahead.

CHAPTER FIVE

THE DOOLITTLE RAID

Hornet and her escort sailed in a zigzag formation similar to the pattern previously used by the *Vincennes* and *Cimarron* while escorting the WS 12X Convoy. The sailors remained at General Quarters from dawn 'til dusk and on call at all times. With the absence of air cover, defense of the *Hornet* fell to the cruisers and destroyers.

Leaving Pearl Harbor on April 8, 1941, Admiral William "Bull" Halsey and Task Force 16.1 forged through rough seas and rendezvoused with Admiral Mitscher's Task Force 16.2 on April 13. The two fleets combined to form Task Force 16. All ships now sailed under Halsey's overall command as they headed west of the Hawaiian Islands into the Pacific. Rumors as to their destination were put to rest when Halsey signaled they were headed for Tokyo.

After merging, the *Hornet* took the lead as the *Enterprise* fell behind her with tankers *Cimarron* and *Sabine* sandwiched between the two carriers. The *Vincennes* and *Northampton* were to one side and the *Nashville* and *Salt Lake City* on the other. Admiral Raymond Spruance commanded the essential cruisers. The destroyers were screening for submarines, with not only the usual outer protection, but with a close eye on the tankers as well.

Meanwhile, negative news from Southeast Asia continued to pour in during the month of April. Bataan had surrendered on April 9, 1942. General Jonathan Wainwright and some 35,000 men escaped to Corregidor Island and defied the Japanese from there. The Bataan Death March began on April 10. Thousands of American and Filipino soldiers died on the forced march. The Allies, and especially America, needed a morale boost, which the Doolittle Raid was designed to provide.

With the merging of the two task forces, the *Enterprise* planes now provided crucial air cover. While the additional cruisers and destroyers gave Task Force 16 a formidable punch, their intrusion into the Japanese-controlled waters of the Pacific would become an obvious threat to the enemy.

The next day, April 14, Jimmy Doolittle called the men together and introduced the pilots to Lt. Commander Stephen Jurika, one of the executive officers on the *Hornet.* Having been a previous U.S. Naval Attaché in Japan, Jurika gave a series of lectures, explaining the differing political ideologies of China and Japan. The Lieutenant described in detail the various military uniforms and dress of both countries and the differences between military and peasant classes. While Doolittle planned the line of attack, the pilots reviewed maps of the cities, and Jurika pointed out specific landmarks; rivers, lakes, bridges, railroads, highways, and other geographical features.

Task Force 16 proceeded without incident despite formidable weather in the Pacific. The rough seas, high winds, and intermittent rain squalls made it difficult for the sailors on the cruisers, destroyers, and especially the tankers. Carrying millions of gallons of fuel, the tankers *Cimarron* and *Sabine* were vital to the mission—and the most vulnerable.

Around 6:30 a.m., April 15, the *Cimarron* came along the port side of the *Hornet* topping off the carrier with fuel for the final run. The tanker then refueled the *Northampton* and *Salt Lake City* while the *Sabine* topped off the *Enterprise*, *Vincennes,* and *Nashville.*

A thousand miles from Tokyo, the *Hornet* was 1,500 yards ahead of the *Enterprise* with *Vincennes* and *Northampton* starboard and the *Salt Lake City* and *Nashville* to port. The slow oilers, unable to keep pace with the carriers, were now left behind with the destroyers for protection. Mitscher summoned Doolittle to the bridge, and informed him "it's time we held that little ceremony we talked about."

On the *Hornet*, peace memorial medals, previously awarded to U.S. military officials by Imperial Japan, were attached to the tail end of the impending bombs. Some bombs had sarcastic greetings written on them as "payback" for Pearl Harbor. With news reels rolling to record the ceremony, Doolittle himself tied a medal onto one of the 500-pounders.

During this time, General Joseph Stillwell was in China collaborating with Generalissimo Chiang Kai-Shek to prepare the cities of Chuchow and Chungking as friendly landing sites since the bombers could not return to the *Hornet*. Other Chinese airfields were also put on alert and prepared for possible landings for the raiders. Stillwell wired Washington that they were "as ready as possible."

Now less than a 1,000 miles of Japan, Task Force 16 continued to encounter swollen seas, increasing gales, and driving rains. Tension was mounting on every ship, especially the *Hornet* and her escort, *Vincennes*. Two U.S. submarines, the *Trout* and *Thresher*, trolling near Tokyo, were reporting weather conditions and scouting for the presence of any Japanese ships in the vicinity. At 3:00 a.m. on April 18, 1942, radar from the *Enterprise* detected two Japanese vessels 12 miles away. General Quarters was called, directing the fleet to quickly change course to avoid discovery.

At 5:00 a.m., search planes were launched in intervals as combat, inner air patrols, and dive bombers screened the seas for Japanese pickets. Radios on the ships were silenced. Communication alerts between planes and ships were now made by the dropping of bean bags from overhead planes onto their decks. At 6:00 a.m., Lt. O. B. Wiseman dropped his bean bag onto the *Enterprise*. An enemy picket was spotted 40 miles dead ahead. The task force reverted back to its original course.

Hubert B. Gibbons, Seaman First Class, was in charge of the lookout station on the *Vincennes*. Looking to port across the bow of the Hornet, he spotted the Nitto Maru, a 70-ton Japanese patrol vessel. Immediately, he phoned in her range and bearing, and signal flags went aloft alerting the fleet. But it was too late. The Nitto had already radioed an attack warning to her flagship. The Japanese were now in search of the American carriers.

Armed with machine guns and one cannon, the *Nitto Maru* hopelessly engaged the carriers. The *Nashville* fired back as planes from the *Enterprise* closed in and finished her off. The Japanese Captain committed seppuku (suicide ritual according to the Japanese Bushido Code of Honor) rather than be captured. Five of the 11 crew survived and were picked up by the *Nashville*.

Knowing they had been discovered, Admiral Halsey had only one option: launch immediately—ten hours early and 200 miles farther from Japan than originally planned. He flagged Mitscher to begin the launch.

Doolittle asked Halsey to proceed ahead another hour and a half while his pilots prepared their planes for launch. After re-spotting to allow for engine start and warm-ups, Doolittle's leading bomber had just over 450 feet of take-off distance. The weather continued to worsen, and the waves sent water cascading over the deck. Heavy rains pelted the pilots as they rushed toward their planes.

On the bridge of the *Hornet*, Doolittle shook Captain Mitscher's hand and running down the ladder, shouted, "Let's go, boys!" The klaxon horn sounded, followed by the announcement: "Army pilots, man your planes!"

The *Hornet* was brought up to full speed and turned into the wind. The moment of truth had arrived for her 16 Mitchell bombers as the blocks were pulled from under the wheels and gas tanks topped off.

The *Hornet* was now rocking like a seesaw, plunging deep into the water each time the bow dipped downward. Doolittle, first to launch his B-25, rose into the sky at 8:20 a.m. Each remaining plane timed their upsurge as the bow of the carrier rose up with each crest of the mountainous waves, in order to get as much boost as possible for takeoff.

The final plane, nicknamed "The Bat Out of Hell," had her tail section protruding over the *Hornet's* stern as she prepared to launch. Back draft from the propellers of the fifteenth plane caused "The Bat" to tilt with her nose up in the air and her tail pointing down toward the water below. As sailors rushed out to bring her nose down, Seaman Bob Wall slipped on the wet deck into the left propeller, mangling his arm. Distracted by the mishap, the pilot, Lt. Bill Farrow, put his wing flaps in the wrong position. With great skill and determination, Farrow was able to clear the last plane from the *Hornet's* storm-swept deck.

Finally, all B-25s were airborne and after circling around the ship, headed in formation toward Tokyo. From their vantage point on the *Vincennes*, E. J. Ridgeway and his fellow gunners witnessed the grandeur of the Mitchell planes successfully taking flight off the *Hornet's* deck, destined for America's first retaliation against the Japanese homeland.

The *Hornet's* hangars lifted her planes for launch to provide air cover for Task Force 16. The fleet reversed course and steamed toward the awaiting destroyers and tankers for their race back to Pearl Harbor. Halsey later called the mission, "One of the most courageous deeds in military history."

The Jimmy Doolittle Bomber Raid was a success, but not without great loss for the pilots and their aircraft. The raiders fought constant headwinds as they hugged the waves of the Pacific at low speed to conserve fuel. Doolittle, alone in his thoughts, began to wonder about the landing arrangements. Chiang Kai-shek, political and military leader of the Republic of China, did not want the American planes to land in his country for fear of retribution from the Japanese army who had a legacy of slaughtering civilians thought to have aided the enemy. Americans in China warned that leaks of classified information were the norm. To avoid this possibility, it was decided that Chiang Kai-shek would not be notified until after the *Hornet's* planes were launched.

Gas consumption was everyone's concern, and a constant check was maintained. As the bombers neared Japan, the weather cleared, giving improved visibility. Landfall was made about 80 miles north of Inubo Shima around noon, Tokyo time, enabling them to get a navigational fix. Since Doolittle was north of his target, he decided to approach from that direction and avoid the anti-aircraft batteries known to be in the western area.

Flying low over the fields as they approached Tokyo, Doolittle's raiders evaded Japanese fighters above, but began receiving flak from anti-aircraft fire below. Closing in, Doolittle spotted a large factory near his first target, so he elevated his plane and opened the bomb doors. Four incendiaries dropped in quick succession, finishing off the strikes, then Doolittle dropped down to ground level and began his escape. Upon reaching the coast of Japan, Doolittle plotted his course and turned west toward China. Immediately he was confronted by headwinds.

The crew checked gas consumption and reserves. Doolittle's plane now had enough fuel to take him 135 miles off China. He was flying low enough to see sharks in the water, when what had been a headwind transformed into a tailwind of 25 mph. Perhaps ditching could be avoided.

Weather conditions worsened and darkness fell on the Doolittle crew as they approached the coast of China. To avoid the mountains that lay ahead, the B-25 increased altitude until only occasional lights below were seen, but no identifying landmarks. Attempted contact with Chuchow was unsuccessful, and without a ground radio to hone in on, landing was not possible. With fuel running low and no other options, the plane was set on automatic pilot. The crew prepared to parachute.

As the needle on the gas gauge edged toward "zero," Doolittle gave the parachute order for the crew: Braemer, Potter, Leonard, and then Cole. By jumping in a straight line, it would be easier to find each other on the ground.

After being in the air thirteen hours, and having traveled over 2,000 miles, Doolittle parachuted last. Having broken both ankles in a previous jump, he quickly decided to bend his legs to avoid the shock.

60

Expecting to hit the ground hard, he was surprised there wasn't much impact. Doolittle soon discovered he had landed in a pungent smelling rice paddy freshly fertilized with night soil, a mixture of manure and water.

Of the sixteen B-25s, each containing five crew members, eleven of the air crews parachuted, four crews crash landed with their planes, and one rerouted to Vladivostok, Russia. Of the entire 80-member air crew, 64 would return to the States, many through India. Ted Lawson's loss of a leg was the worst injury. The five crew members that rerouted to Russia were detained but later escaped through Iran. Two crew members were killed in crashes, one perished after parachuting, and eight were captured by the Japanese. Three of the captured were executed: Lt. Dean Hallmark, Sgt. Harold Spatz, and Lt. Bill Farrow. Lt. John Meder died in captivity, and the remaining four, Corporal Jacob DeShazer, Lt. Robert Hite, Lt. Chase Nielson, and Lt. George Barr were released at war's end.

The bombing changed the climate of the war. Chiang Kai-shek's worst fears were realized. An estimated 200,000 Chinese, thought to have aided the Americans, were slaughtered by the Japanese.

Though the actual damage from the bombing was minimal, the raid's psychological effect on the shocked citizens of Japan was enormous. They had been assured by Emperor Hirohito that no bombs would ever be dropped on their homeland.

Of course, when news of the raid hit America, the public was elated. Doolittle, however, felt the mission had been a complete failure. All sixteen B-25s were lost. It seemed to him Leavenworth Prison would be his future destination. Expecting to be court marshalled upon his arrival back to the States, the surprised Lieutenant Colonel was awarded the Medal of Honor by President Roosevelt, immediately upgraded to Brigadier General, and heralded as an American war hero.

Later asked of the origin of the Doolittle Bombers, President Roosevelt cryptically replied, "Shangri-La." Unable to find such a location on the maps, Admiral Yamamoto concluded that the raiders had come from Midway and set in motion ambitious plans to capture that island, and even Pearl Harbor.

After launching the Doolittle bombers, the *Hornet* and *Enterprise* groups reunited with their tankers and escorting destroyers, and the combined groups, under the command of Admiral Halsey, proceeded to Pearl Harbor, arriving April 25, 1942. En route, the Task Force received a report that Radio Tokyo was in a state of confusion. They knew then that Doolittle's raiders had struck their targets.

USS *Vincennes* had yet to fire upon the enemy, but being a part of the WS 12X Convoy and Task Force 16 that escorted Doolittle's planes for the first attack on the Japanese homeland, were accomplishments few could claim.

CHAPTER SIX

CORAL SEA AND PRELUDE TO MIDWAY

Coral Sea Battle

The first real test of strength between Japan and the United States would be in the Coral Sea and the Solomon Islands. The carriers USS *Yorktown* and USS *Lexington*, and their escorts had been in that area since February 1942. The *Lexington* had raided Rabaul, and both carriers had attacked Japanese bases at Lae and Salamaua on New Guinea. When the opposing fleets engaged on May 8, the battle would be fought entirely by carrier planes from both sides. It was the first aircraft carrier battle in history, and neither surface fleet spotted the other during the battle.

Japanese Battle Plan

To seize control of the Coral Sea and strengthen defense of their major naval base at Rabaul, in late April 1942, the Japanese developed plans to invade and occupy Tulagi in the southeastern Solomon Islands. This move would provide support for their attack on Port Moresby, a vital outpost in the Australian-held territory of Papua, New Guinea. The complex plan, code-named "Operation MO" (Operation Moresby Occupation), centered around their Port Morseby Invasion Force that included several supporting thrusts.

First was the invasion of Tulagi, where a seaplane base would be established for patrol and reconnaissance of the southern Solomon Islands. A Japanese covering fleet, which included the light carrier, *Shoho*, would depart from Truk to protect the Tulagi invasion force. Fleet carriers *Shokaku* and *Zuikaku*, based at Truk, would sortie with the main strike force along the northern coastline of the Solomon Islands, which would serve as a protective screen for the fleet from the American carriers.

Anticipating the U.S. fleet would attack the Tulagi force, the strike force would close in with the covering force and the light carrier *Shoho* to defeat the American and Australian navies in the Coral Sea. The Port Morseby invasion force would then be free to move on and take the city. With the elimination of the Allied navies in the Coral Sea, and the occupation of Papau, New Guinea and the Solomon Islands,

Australia and New Zealand would be open for invasion or possibly forced to sue for peace.

Japanese Forces

Carrier Strike Force: Carriers *Shokaku* and *Zuikaku*, heavy cruisers *Myoko* and *Haguro*, six destroyers and one tanker.

Port Morseby Covering/Landing Forces: Light carrier *Shoho*, heavy cruisers *Aoba, Kako, Kinugasa,* and *Furutaka*, light cruisers *Yubari, Tenyru,* and *Tatsuta*, seven destroyers, one minelayer, four gunboats, one patrol boat, twelve transports and auxiliary craft.

Tulagi Invasion Force: Two destroyers, two minelayers, one transport and auxiliary craft.

American Intelligence Discovers Japanese Plan

During this time, U.S. intelligence, under the leadership of cryptanalyst Joseph Rochefort, had been intercepting Japanese radio traffic that used coded letters to identify bases, ports, and installations. Rochefort, an expert Japanese linguist, was assigned to break the Imperial Japanese Navy's most secure cipher system which would allow the U.S. Navy to know where and when Japan would strike next. Captain Rochefort and his group had decoded the message "MO" and rightly believed the target to be Port Moresby in New Guinea.

Allied/American Forces

<u>Task Group 17.2 – Attack Group</u>: Cruisers USS *Minneapolis, New Orleans, Astoria, Chester,* and *Portland* and five destroyers

<u>Task Group 17.5 – Carrier Group</u>: Carriers *Yorktown* and *Lexington,* and four destroyers

<u>Task Group 17.3 – Support Group</u>: Cruisers HMAS *Australia* and *Hobart,* and USS *Chicago,* and two destroyers

By May 3, the Japanese had occupied Tulagi. The following day, Admiral Fletcher's force, including the two aircraft carriers, *Lexington* and *Yorktown,* gave the Japanese a surprise attack at Tulagi, sinking several enemy ships and shooting down several planes. By bringing in seaplane tenders, the Japanese quickly established a port at Tulagi.

The American and Japanese fleets continued their mutual searches. On May 7, Japanese reconnaissance planes discovered some U.S. ships, mistakenly identified as a carrier and escorting cruiser. The Japanese rushed over 50 planes toward what turned out to be a flat-topped tanker and its escort destroyer. Overwhelmed by the onslaught, the destroyer was sunk and the tanker was left burning. Meanwhile, to the northwest, American planes targeted and sank the Japanese light carrier *Shoho.* In spite of these initial encounters, the two carrier forces were still unsure of the other's location.

The respective scouts spotted their prey on the morning of May 8 and the battle began. Japanese planes targeted and sank the U.S. carrier *Lexington* and did serious damage to the carrier *Yorktown*. American dive bombers and torpedo bombers managed to inflict moderate damage on the Japanese carrier *Shokaku*, and destroyed a large number of *Zuikaku's* planes and experienced pilots.

To aid Fletcher's force, Admiral Halsey rushed from Pearl Harbor with the *Vincennes, Enterprise, Hornet,* and other escorts. They arrived late afternoon of the second day of battle—too late to participate in the fight. However, their presence encouraged their American comrades and discouraged the enemy.

Due to heavy losses in aircraft and carriers, the two adversaries left the battle. With most of their aircraft depleted, the Japanese, now without air cover, were forced to cancel their Port Moresby invasion.

The Coral Sea Battle was the first time the Allies confronted and stopped advancing Japanese forces. The Imperial Navy thought they had sunk two American carriers, not knowing the damaged *Yorktown* had returned to Pearl Harbor for repairs. Japanese losses were one light carrier (*Shoho*) sunk, 1 destroyer, 3 small warships, 92 aircraft, with damage to the carrier *Shokaku*, 1 destroyer, and 1 transport. Almost 1,000 Japanese were killed. Allied losses were one carrier sunk (*Lexington*), one carrier damaged (*Yorktown*), one oiler and one destroyer sunk. U.S. Naval records indicate 543 Allies killed.

Although the two carriers, *Shokaku* and *Zuikaku*, would be unavailable for immediate action, the IJN continued their plans for a secret attack on Midway Island. Meanwhile, Captain Rochefort in Hawaii was still intercepting coded messages.

American Intelligence Discovers Plan to Attack Midway

Not surprisingly, the cryptanalysts under Captain Joseph John Rochefort were instrumental in discovering Yamamoto's plans to attack Midway Island. Hidden away in the basement of an administration building at Pearl Harbor's Naval District, Rochefort's intelligence team worked endless hours in what they referred to as "the dungeon." Just days before the December 7 attack on Pearl Harbor, the unit had deciphered only a small portion of the Japanese code which hinted at a possible aggression against the U.S. naval base at Hawaii. Determined to prevent another surprise attack, Rochefort spent days on end in his bunker, resolved to decode the Japanese radio traffic.

By March 1942, Rochefort and his team were able to track the messages from the Japanese warships and maintained that an upcoming attack would be in the Central Pacific. The boys in the "dungeon" had aligned the codes with the decrypts, and Rochefort was certain code-group "AF" referred to Midway. The codebreakers in Washington were convinced otherwise, believing the next target would be elsewhere, possibly the Aleutians, New Guinea, or even the west coast of the United States.

Rochefort's group, still convinced that "AF" was indeed Midway, received permission to radio an emergency message reporting a faked shortage of fresh water on the island. The Japanese codebreakers took the bait and relayed the intercepted warning to their navy, requesting water desalination equipment be sent to target "AF" on June 4 and 5, 1942. Rochefort was vindicated. Now he was not only certain of the planned attack on Midway, but he even had the dates. After Washington Intelligence was convinced of the target and dates, Admiral Nimitz in Hawaii set in motion plans to defend the U.S. naval base at Midway, two small islands at the extreme northwest end of the Northern Hawaiian Chain—approximately 1,300 miles from Oahu.

The American defense at Midway would hinge on the ability of two carrier task forces to find and destroy the Japanese fleet. Therefore, Nimitz first had to deal with the recent losses to his fleet at the Coral Sea Battle. The *Lexington* had been sunk and the *Yorktown* was soon to be in dry dock at Pearl Harbor for an estimated repair time of three months. He ordered the *Yorktown* to be readied for battle in three days. Thousands of dock yard men worked day and night to have the carrier sea-worthy by the deadline.

Next on the list was the chain of command and establishment of the Pacific Fleet Task Force. Admiral William "Bull" Halsey had been hospitalized at Pearl Harbor due to a severe case of shingles. Halsey recommended that Admiral Raymond Spruance, his cruiser commander, replace him for the Midway assignment. Nimitz agreed.

U.S. Pacific Fleet Task Force

Admiral Chester W. Nimitz, Commander-in-Chief, U.S. Pacific Fleet

Admiral Frank Jack Fletcher, Overall Commander, Combined U.S. Pacific Task Forces (TF 16 and 17)

Admiral Raymond Spruance, Commander, U.S. Pacific Task Force 16

Carrier Group: USS *Enterprise* and *Hornet*

Cruiser Group: USS *Vincennes, Pensacola, Northampton, New Orleans, Minneapolis,* and *Atlanta*

Destroyer Screen: Nine destroyers

Oilers Group: Four oilers

Admiral Frank Jack Fletcher, Commander, U.S. Pacific Task Force 17

Carrier Group: USS *Yorktown*

Cruiser Group: USS *Astoria* and *Portland*

Destroyer Screen: Six destroyers

Japanese Forces

Admiral Isoroku Yamamoto, Commander of Japanese Combined Fleet

First Fleet Main Force, Admiral Yamamoto, Commander

Consisted of seven battleships, three light cruisers, two sea plane carriers, one light carrier, and 20 destroyers. Attached to the Main Force was four carriers, two battleships, three cruisers, and 11 destroyers commanded by Vice Admiral Chuichi Nagumo.

Midway Invasion Force, Vice Admiral Nobutake Kondo, Commander

Consisted of two battleships, four heavy cruisers, one light carrier, and seven destroyers. Subordinate to Kondo was the Midway Occupation force, commanded by Rear Admiral Raizo Tanaka, and consisting of 12 transports with about 5,000 troops and a screen of one light cruiser, 10 destroyers, and three patrol boats.

Midway Support Force, Vice Admiral Takeo Kurita, Commander
Consisted of four heavy cruisers and two destroyers

Northern Area Force, Admiral Yamamoto, Overall Commander (Aleutians)
Consisted of one heavy carrier, one light carrier, two cruisers, three destroyers, and an invasion fleet of four transports carrying about 1,000 soldiers accompanied by seven destroyers.

Yamamoto knew the Americans would be compelled to vigorously defend their vital Pearl Harbor outpost at Midway. He divided his forces in a battle plan that included an attack on the Aleutian Islands in hopes of luring the U.S. Fleet away from Midway into a fatally compromised situation. Unknown to Yamamoto, the Americans had discovered when and where he would attack next, and that the carrier *Yorktown*, thought to have been sunk at Coral Sea, would also be in the fight.

On the morning of May 27, 1942, four of the five Imperial Japanese naval forces, under the command of Admiral Chuichi Nagumo, sailed from Hashirajima. By nightfall, the forces entered the Pacific headed for Midway. The Aleutians Invasion Force sortied from

Ominato, Japan, and headed north on May 28, for the diversion attack on the Alaskan Islands. From the south, the Japanese Invasion and Support Forces, sortied from the Marianas. Last to leave port on May 29, was Yamamoto's First Fleet Main Force.

In preparation for the oncoming invasion, Nimitz deployed submarines from Pearl Harbor for reconnaissance. Midway's garrison was reinforced to approximately 3,000 men, the island's anti-aircraft batteries were strengthened, and large numbers of Catalina flying boats began patrolling the area daily.

Meanwhile, the Japanese began their own reconnaissance. An advanced submarine force raced toward Hawaii to set up a picket north of Pearl Harbor, but their watch would be in vain. Upon their arrival on June 3, Task Force 16, with the *Vincennes* in the group, had already left Pearl Harbor on May 29, followed by Task Force 17 on May 30. Both American fleets had disappeared into the Pacific unobserved.

Aleutians Diversion by the Japanese

The Japanese Northern decoy force headed for the Aleutians through the North Pacific on June 2, 1942. Though the Alaskan islands were strategic to the United States, they were lightly manned with the only forces of any significance stationed at Dutch Harbor. In anticipation of the enemy's attack, the Americans flew continual reconnaissance, but due to poor weather and low visibility, failed to locate the invaders. The Japanese struck the islands, inflicting damage on Dutch Harbor. Japanese troops quickly occupied Kiska and Attu over the next few days, creating a problem the Americans would have to tackle the following year. The attempt to draw the U.S. carriers away from Midway Island had failed.

While the Japanese Northern Force launched their diversionary attack on the Aleutians, Admiral Nagumo's carrier strike force was steaming toward Midway, followed by Yamamoto's main force of battleships about 200 miles to the rear. Also approaching from the southwest was the Japanese Invasion Force.

By June 3, Midway's Catalina flying boats were reconnoitering a large area of the Pacific Ocean to cover all likely enemy approaches to Midway Island. That morning a PBY sighted Admiral Tanaka's Occupation Force west-southwest of Midway, but mistakenly reported it as the Main Force. B-17s took off from Midway just after noon and found Tanaka's transports two hours later. Amidst heavy AA gunfire, the American planes dropped their bombs but failed to make any hits.

Later, another Catalina sighted a large formation of invading ships and reported their bearing and range. The Japanese Invasion Force was 700 miles away. Midway's B-17 bombers were armed and ready. The commanders on the island delayed launching their planes until further confirmation was received of the fast approaching ships.

Two hours later, reports were passed on to the Task Forces 16 and 17, waiting over 300 miles northeast of Midway. The Japanese main body had been sighted to the southwest. Relying on his intelligence sources that this was only the invasion force, Admiral Nimitz signaled the Midway commanders that the Japanese carrier strike force would not hit until the following day. At dawn of June 4,

Midway Catalinas were again sent out for reconnaissance. Learning from their past mistakes at Pearl Harbor, the Americans ordered Midway's B-17s to takeoff so they would not be caught on the ground.

CHAPTER SEVEN

ATTACK ON MIDWAY

Just before dawn on June 4, 1942, Admiral Nagumo launched his first wave of 108 planes with dive bombers, torpedo bombers, and Zero fighters in equal numbers. Following Japanese Naval Code, Nagumo kept half his aircraft in reserve should any American warships be discovered, though he thought it highly unlikely. As soon as the strike wave was aloft, reconnaissance planes were sent out, but laboring through bad weather and poor visibility, they were insufficient for the task. The Admiral's miscalculation of his enemy's presence would later prove fatal to his carrier fleet.

As the Japanese scouts were taking off, Midway's Catalinas (PBYs) were leaving the island on their own search and around 5:30 a.m., one PBY spotted two Japanese carriers. The Japanese carrier strike force was exactly where Admiral Nimitz had anticipated.

Catalinas then reported Nagumo's first wave of Zero fighters approaching Midway.

The Japanese planes, still several miles from their target, were picked up by Midway's radar. Bombers, remaining on the island, flew out without escort to search for the Japanese carriers while the fighters stayed in close in defense of Midway's naval base. Outmanned and outgunned, the Marine fighters slammed into the enemy force, but after brushing the American defenders aside, the Japanese bombers and torpedo planes broke through only to meet well-placed AA fire on Midway. Taking some losses, but finding no planes on the ground, Japanese raiders targeted Sand Island's airstrip and bombed the oil tanks. Eastern Island was next in line and after finishing their mission, the enemy raiders returned to their carriers. Of the original 108 Japanese planes, 11 were shot down and more than 40 damaged. Marine fighters suffered heavy losses.

The raid on Midway failed to accomplish its objective. The Japanese strike leader radioed Nagumo that the airfield was still intact and capable of refueling and launching American bombers. A second strike would be necessary before sending their invasion troops ashore.

As the first Japanese strike wave returned from Midway, and while Nagumo planned a second strike, Midway's B-26s and torpedo bombers found his carriers. Zero fighters of the CAP (Japanese Combat Air Patrol) zoomed in to confront the bombers, who targeted the carrier *Akagi*. Heavy gunfire took down many of the Midway planes, including a B-26 that crashed into the sea barely missing the

Akagi's bridge and Nagumo's staff. The Americans failed to register any hits and their losses were staggering.

A shaken Nagumo ordered a second strike creating the need to exchange the anti-ship ordnance already installed on the reserve torpedo planes. The dive bombers were unarmed, but the torpedo planes had to be refitted with general purpose bombs designed for use against land targets. Admiral Yamamoto had ordered the reserve force to be armed in anticipation of the American warships in the area. Disregarding these orders, torpedo planes were in the process of ordnance change when Nagumo received an alarming report at a most inopportune time. An American naval force had been spotted to the east, but his scout gave no details as to its composition.

During this time, three more failed attacks from Midway were made on Nagumo's carriers by 16 dive bombers at 7:55 a.m., 17 B-17s at 8:10 a.m., and 11 more dive bombers at 8:20 a.m. The Admiral quickly reversed orders and demanded additional information regarding the enemy ships. Thirty minutes passed before he was notified of a single carrier and a supporting surface fleet.

While the Japanese carrier force had been engaging Midway's bombers, the *Enterprise* and *Hornet* were preparing to attack. The *Vincennes* was with the carriers and cruisers over 300 miles to the northeast of Midway at a destination code-named "Point Luck" awaiting the advance of the powerful Japanese armada. Dad recalled this moment while we were watching the movie, Midway, "We knew we were outnumbered. I prayed for God's help as our planes launched." Admiral Spruance had sent his fighters, torpedo bombers and dive bombers aloft. He held 36 fighters in reserve for defense.

Yorktown, thirty miles to the rear, with her scout planes now recovered, closed the gap and launched her planes. While the Japanese were able to launch a coordinated strike force of 108 aircraft in only seven minutes, it had taken the *Enterprise* and *Hornet* an hour to launch 117. Consequently, the American squadrons rushed off piecemeal toward their targets in several different groups. By 9 a.m., over 150 American planes from the three carriers were on a search-and-destroy mission.

Captain Miles Browning of the *Enterprise* estimated that the Japanese carriers were 175 miles away, if Nagumo remained on course. But Nagumo changed courses just as *Yorktown* launched her planes. His CAP of Zero fighters now needed to land and refuel, along with his circling Midway strike force. Nagumo had to make a decision and fast. Should he land his Midway attackers and send a second strike, or rearm and go after the American carrier?

In the confusion, the carrier decks were in chaos. Armed strike planes filled the hangar decks with fuel hoses stretched across the decks during the hasty refueling operations. Because of the repeated change in ordnance, there was no time for safety procedures. Instead, bombs and torpedoes were strewn around the hangars and decks, rather than safely stowed in the magazines. Nagumo decided to land his Midway strike force, and, after arming his reserve with anti-ship armament, attack the carrier. But it was too late. The American planes were fast approaching.

An air group from the *Hornet* followed a wrong heading, but one squadron broke away and found Nagumo's carriers. Fifteen torpedo planes attacked at 9:25 a.m., scoring no hits and were annihilated. Just five minutes later, 14 torpedo planes from the Enterprise attacked, with the same results. As Nagumo's deck crews scurried to land the Midway strike planes at 10:00 a.m., a third attack came from *Yorktown*—they also missed their targets. By now, the Zeros were low on fuel and ammunition and had been drawn out of their covering position.

Five Minutes that Changed the Battle

Nagumo was about to signal his planes for take-off when suddenly, dive bombers bore down on his carriers. Wade McClusky's two squadrons from the *Enterprise* and Max Leslie's squadron from the *Yorktown* arrived in perfect synchronicity. The determined McClusky had continued to search for the enemy ships and by divine providence, spotted the wake of a Japanese destroyer rushing back to join Nagumo's fleet. The Japanese carriers were about to be obliterated by the American dive bombers.

According to William Koenig's timeline, 30 *Enterprise* dive bombers from Wade McClusky's squadrons headed toward the carriers *Kaga* and *Akagi* at 10:25 a.m. *Kaga* was the first target. Blasted four or five times with direct hits, she sustained heavy damage and multiple fires. One bomb landed near her bridge, killing the captain and his senior officers.

Akagi, Admiral Nagumo's flagship, was the next target. One direct hit from Lt. Richard Best's squadron was the fatal blow. The bomb struck the carrier's flight deck landing in the middle of her armed and fueled aircraft preparing for lift-off. The flames raged forward to Nagumo's battle station and he was forced to transfer his flag to a cruiser.

Almost simultaneously, Max Leslie's squadron from the *Yorktown* dove on the *Soryu* scoring three hits and causing extensive damage. The carrier's waiting strike force was annihilated by the third hit to her deck.

In a little over five minutes, three of the four carriers from the mightiest carrier fleet in existence were burning out of control. Admiral Nimitz would later recount that McClusky's continued search, and the resulting actions, were the turning point in the battle for the American fleet at Midway.

In less than 30 minutes, the lone aircraft carrier *Hiryu,* counterattacked. Her first strike wave, consisting of eighteen dive bombers and six Zeros, followed the retreating Americans. At 11:30 a.m., the *Yorktown* launched ten scout planes to search for the *Hiryu.* Meanwhile, attackers from the *Hiryu* spotted the *Yorktown.* The strike planes were met by a hail of fire from *Yorktown's* fighter defenses, and ten were shot down, but the remaining 14 planes continued their descent upon the U.S. carrier. Five enemy planes survived the return fire from *Yorktown* and her support ships. Then three torpedo planes from the *Hiryu* zoomed in from the north, and *Yorktown's* Wildcats from the CAP splashed one of them.

During the maelstrom, the *Yorktown* took three hits and was heavily damaged, forcing Admiral Fletcher to move his command staff to the heavy cruiser *Astoria.* The spreading fires were quickly put out, and repair teams patched her up. Unknown to the Japanese, *Yorktown* was now able to resume air operations.

Vincennes and *Pensacola*, with accompanying destroyers, *Benham* and *Balch*, were quickly dispatched to form a protective screen around the crippled *Yorktown*. Heavy cruisers *Astoria* and *Portland* were on the *Yorktown's* starboard and port bows, as the *Vincennes* and *Pensacola* moved in on her starboard and port quarters. Destroyers *Benham* and *Balch* positioned between the cruisers.

An hour later, *Hiryu* launched her second wave, a scratch force of ten torpedo bombers (Kates) and six escorts. Task Force 17's radar soon picked them up when 15 miles out, and *Yorktown* launched planes to intercept. American Wildcats attacked the raiders and splashed one Kate. Nine torpedo bombers survived and swept into the enemy attack. Five more Japanese torpedo bombers were shot down by anti-aircraft fire, but not before four were able to launch their torpedoes.

The *Yorktown*, now under her own steam and no longer belching smoke, was mistaken by the Japanese for one of her undamaged companion carriers, and was hit again. Two torpedoes struck her port side. After one of the raiders made a suicide dive and crashed onto *Yorktown's* deck, she exploded. Losing all power, the carrier began listing to port.

During the sharp, bitter action, *Vincennes* opened fire on the Kates approaching from the port side. Increasing speed and slowly turning to starboard, *Vincennes* kept her port guns trained on the enemy and bagged one Kate.

At 3:00 p.m., the *Yorktown's* crew received orders to abandon ship. The Japanese had left the damaged *Yorktown*, thinking they had put a second American carrier out of the fight. But the playing field was not as level as they thought—the IJN lost three of their four carriers, and only one American carrier was destroyed.

While *Yorktown's* crew was being rescued by the *Vincennes* and attending destroyers, *Hiryu* was spotted a hundred miles northwest of the dying *Yorktown*. At 3:30 p.m., the *Enterprise* launched a final strike wave of 24 dive bombers. Four bombs hit the *Hiryu* while she recovered and refueled her last remaining aircraft for a third strike against the American carriers. She was left ablaze and most of her pilots were lost.

Admiral Nagumo's last carrier was finished.

Undaunted by news of the Midway catastrophe, Admiral Yamamoto held fast to his goal of bringing the Americans to their knees. His battleships and cruisers still had awesome firepower, and the Japanese had the edge in night fighting. Realizing he was incapable of forcing a battle before daylight the next day, Yamamoto's fleet retreated from the area. He would fight another day, another time. Meanwhile, the American carriers sailed out of the battle area that evening.

Efforts to salvage the damaged *Yorktown* looked favorable until late afternoon of June 6, when a Japanese submarine slipped through the debris-covered waters, and let loose a torpedo spread. Two struck the *Yorktown*. A third struck the destroyer USS *Hammann*, which had been providing auxiliary power to the *Yorktown*. *Hammann* sank taking 80 lives with her. Few casualties were incurred on the *Yorktown* as most of her crew had already been evacuated, but further efforts to salvage her were now hopeless. Her remaining repairmen were evacuated, and she sank the morning of June 7.

To the astonishment of the Allies, the Japanese press announced their victory at Midway, and the citizens of Japan and many of the military commanders were kept in the dark about their losses. When the Japanese fleet returned to Hashirajima after the battle, the wounded were hospitalized in isolation wards and placed under quarantine to keep the major defeat a secret from their families. The remaining officers and men were quickly sent to other fleet units without being allowed to see family or friends, then shipped to the South Pacific, where a majority died in battle. An indignant American Press reported the incident, and the American public knew in their hearts that the United States Military would never treat their returning warriors in such an egregious manner.

USS *Vincennes* and E. J. Ridgeway were awarded their first Battle Stars for their participation at Midway.

USS *Vincennes* received some damage while defending the *Yorktown.* Returning to Pearl Harbor, the heavy cruiser was in dry dock for repairs and alterations through early July. She then conducted tactical exercises off the island of Hawaii with Task Force 11 before departing on July 14 to rendezvous with Task Forces 16, 18, and 62.

Slated to participate in the Guadalcanal landings, *Vincennes* joined with Task Force 62 in late July, and conducted landing exercises and bombardment drills off Koro Island in Fiji. After refueling and resupply, *Vincennes* formed up with the American warships headed for the Solomon Islands.

CHAPTER EIGHT

GUADALCANAL CAMPAIGN

August 7, 1942 – February 9, 1943

Nine months to the day from the attack on Pearl Harbor, the United States launched their first offensive—an amphibious campaign against the Japanese. The target: Guadalcanal, part of the Solomon Islands, located in the South Pacific to the northeast of Australia. For the next six months, the mosquito and disease-plagued island, with its surrounding waters, would become a hotly contested war zone.

Japanese Background

In May 1942, Japan occupied Tulagi, a small island on the Solomon Islands. The Japanese quickly began construction of a strategic airfield at Lunga Point on nearby Guadalcanal in early July

1942. From such a base, the Japanese long-range bombers would be able to compromise the sea lanes between the United States West Coast to the populous East Coast of Australia. By August 1942, the Japanese had some 900 naval troops stationed at Tulagi and the nearby islands, as well as 2,800 personnel on Guadalcanal.

United States' Background

By late March of 1942, the United States Joint Chiefs of Staff had divided the Pacific Theater into three areas: Pacific Ocean Areas, the Southwest Pacific Ocean Areas, and the South Pacific Ocean Areas. Admiral Chester Nimitz, Commander in Chief, U.S. Pacific Fleet, was appointed Commander, Pacific Ocean Areas with operational control over all American and Allied units (air, land, and sea) in that area. General Douglas A. MacArthur was appointed Supreme Commander of Allied Forces of the Southwest Pacific Area. Vice Admiral Robert Ghormley, was appointed Commander of the South Pacific Ocean Areas.

In early July 1942, General George Marshall, U.S. Army Chief of Staff, and Admiral Ernest King, Chief of U.S. Fleet and Naval Operations, divided responsibility for upcoming operations in the Pacific between Admiral Nimitz and General MacArthur. Nimitz would first target the Santa Cruz Islands and Tulagi in the Solomons. MacArthur would then capture Lae, Salamaua, and the northeast coast of New Guinea, then attack Rabaul.

When the U.S. Military received an intelligence report indicating the Japanese were close to completing an airfield on

Guadalcanal (one of the larger of the Solomon Islands), the Joint Chiefs of Staff immediately revised their targets. The Navy would bypass Santa Cruz and knock out both Tulagi and Guadalcanal in the first phase, denying the Japanese airfields that would give them control of the surrounding waters. Meanwhile, MacArthur was to plan the follow-up campaigns.

The Americans were unsure of the size of the enemy land forces now occupying Guadalcanal. They had a more exact reconnaissance of Japanese strength to the northwest in the vicinity of New Britain. There lurked the Fourth Inner South Sea Fleet of the Japanese Imperial Navy, commanded by the highly respected Admiral Gunichi Makawa.

Japanese Forces

Rear Admiral Gunichi Mikawa, Commander, Eighth Japanese Fleet
Heavy Cruisers: *Chokai* (Flagship), *Aoba, Furutaka, Kako, Kinugasa*
Light Cruisers: *Tenryu* and *Yubari*
Destroyer: *Yunagi*

Heavy cruiser *Chokai*, Mikawa's flagship, was a 13,000-ton "Leviathan" with ten 8-inch guns and 24 torpedo tubes plus reloads. Under Mikawa was Rear Admiral Aimoto Goto's surface fleet of heavy cruisers, each carrying six 8-inch guns and eight torpedo tubes. All ships carried the 24-inch diameter, 30-foot long, oxygen-driven, half-ton warhead Type 93 torpedo. Later dubbed the "Long Lance," this torpedo had a 490 kg warhead with a maximum range of 40,000 yards and an effective range of 22,000 yards.

In contrast, American torpedoes had many problems. The Mark 15 torpedo, dated from the early 1930's, had a smaller warhead with a maximum range of 15,000 yards and an effective range of 6,000 yards. The Long Lance exploded when it hit its target, while its American counterpart seldom detonated, even when registering hits.

United States/Allied Forces

Vice Admiral Robert L. Ghormley, Commander South Pacific Ocean Areas

Vice Admiral Frank J. Fletcher, Commander Expeditionary Force and Officer in Tactical Command of Task Force 61

Rear Admiral Noyes, Commander of Air Support Force - Task Force 62 (under overall command of Admiral Fletcher)

Rear Admiral Richmond Kelly Turner, Amphibious Force – Task Force 62 (responsible for putting the Marines ashore and off-loading their combat support and supplies)

Royal Navy Rear Admiral V.A.C. Crutchley – Task Force 62 (under Turner's command and responsible for the defensive screen around Guadalcanal)

Savo Island Screening Groups

<u>Western Approach:</u>

<u>Southern Group</u> – RADM Crutchley: Heavy Cruisers HMAS *Australia*, HMAS *Canberra*, and USS *Chicago*, and Destroyers USS *Bagley* and *Patterson*

<u>Northern Group</u> – Captain Riefkohl: Heavy Cruisers USS *Vincennes*, USS *Quincy*, and USS *Astoria*, and Destroyers USS *Helm* and *Wilson*

<u>Radar Pickets</u> – Destroyers USS *Blue* and USS *Ralph Talbot*

<u>Eastern Approach:</u>

<u>Eastern Group</u> – RADM Scott: Light Cruisers USS *San Juan* and HMAS *Hobart*, and Destroyers USS *Monssen* and USS *Buchanan*. (Positioned to guard the entrance to the Sound and Guadalcanal, this group had no part in the engagement on August 9.)

USS Vincennes Prepares for Battle

On the evening of August 5, 1942, Chaplain Schwyhart onboard the USS *Vincennes* led a simple church service that ended with communion. Many of the crew attended—they had no idea this would be the last service held on their ship.

On August 6, 1942, General Quarters was called before sunrise. Thankfully, the skies were overcast, making it difficult for enemy planes to spot the U.S. ships as they formed into their positions for the attack on Guadalcanal and Tulagi.

Actions on August 7 and 8, 1942

At daybreak on August 7, 1942, *Vincennes* sent out her scout planes and then unleashed her main and secondary batteries for shore bombardment. The American invasion was underway. The Marines met little resistance at the beach and advanced steadily inland. They captured the coveted airstrip, renaming it Henderson Field in honor of Major Lofton Henderson, the first Marine aviator killed in action at Midway.

The Japanese defenders alerted their high command, who postponed their planned attack on Allied positions in New Guinea and quickly sent their forces to Guadalcanal. With incredible speed, they began their counterattack on the Americans only hours after the assault. Betty bombers escorted by fighters roared in from Rabaul, and around noon August 7, dogfights erupted all over the sky.

Sunward of the transports, *Vincennes* was among the first ships to open fire. Forced to jettison their deadly loads prematurely, the Japanese planes retired without inflicting damage, but not before *Vincennes* shot down two of them. Two hours later, dive-bombers broke through the CAP and targeted USS *Mugford* while on patrol off Lunga Point. The destroyer took a hit to her after-gun mount, knocking out two of her five-inch guns. The toll on Mugford was eight killed,

17 wounded, and 10 missing. She resumed operations the following day.

At dawn on August 8, the Bettys rushed out from Rabaul with orders to locate and strike the American carrier force. Unable to find the flattops, they turned their attention to the invading ships at Guadalcanal. The enemy planes swooped in from the east, opposite from their base, hoping for a surprise attack. Thanks to coast watchers up the Solomons, the American ships knew of the approaching bombers and lay in wait for the attackers. As soon as they came within range, *Vincennes* opened her five-inch cannons, followed by her 20mm guns, splashing some of the planes while others exploded in the air.

One Betty dodged the AA fire and torpedoed the destroyer *Jarvis*, crippling her; another, in flames, plummeted onto the deck of the transport *George F. Elliot*. With fierce tenacity, the remaining bombers continued their attacks, but *Vincennes* was able to dodge the torpedoes from the Bettys. Then one bomber honed in on the heavy cruiser and fired with reckless determination until hit by AA fire, exploding and splashing into the sea.

Reports of Mikawa's Approaching Ships Delayed

Admiral Frank J. Fletcher, Commander of the Expeditionary Force, commanded three of the four remaining carriers in the U.S. Pacific Fleet. Protection of the three American carriers, now under constant threat from Japanese subs in the area, was paramount.

Fletcher's forces had fought intense Japanese sorties throughout the day on August 8, 1942. The initial amphibious landings at Guadalcanal and Tulagi had gone well, but his carriers had lost over 20 aircraft to Japanese air raids while defending the transports and marine landing forces. The raids disrupted the off-loading of the Army's supplies and support equipment, leaving Fletcher preoccupied by the attack from Japanese bombers and torpedo planes.

Meanwhile, sporadic reports were being received of Mikawa's approaching surface fleet headed down the slot off Bougainville Island on August 8. Combined sightings from various allied submarines and different aerial reconnaissance missions, as well as communication delays between Nimitz and MacArthur's chain-of-command, gave Admiral Turner an incomplete picture of Mikawa's position and strategy for the traditional Japanese night attack.

The evening of August 8, Captain Riefkohl of the *Vincennes* intercepted a message sent to Admiral Turner, Commander of the Allied naval force off Guadalcanal, and gave a briefing to his senior officers. Around noon that day, Japanese warships had been spotted by an Australian Hudson reconnaissance plane that reported the fleet was headed their way. The tardiness of the report (due to no fault of the Hudson), as well as the description of the fleet (three cruisers, three destroyers, and two sea plane tenders) would later cause all of the commanders at Guadalcanal much consternation and surprise in the early morning hours of August 9.

As the sun set on August 8, few aboard the *Vincennes*, or any other U.S. ship, expected a night attack.

Mikawa's Plan of Attack

Though outnumbered, Mikawa's ships packed a punch unmatched by the American fleet. The Japanese realized early on that they could not equal America's industrial output ship-for-ship. To gain an advantage, they became specialists in night attacks using searchlights, torpedoes, and improved ship-to-ship communication in the dark. They also developed night binoculars that allowed look-outs to sight ships up to 20,000 yards away.

Mikawa's plan was to approach the south side of Savo Island in darkness and torpedo the Allied ships off Guadalcanal. Next, the Japanese would turn east and north and destroy the Tulagi landing force with torpedoes and guns. Mikawa's ships would then proceed to the north side of Savo Island and depart the area before the American carriers could counter with an air attack at daylight.

Admiral Fletcher Requests to Withdraw His Carriers

As Mikawa sailed out of Rabaul for his stealth approach toward Savo Island, Admiral Fletcher radioed Admiral Ghormley, requesting permission to withdraw his carriers due to recent aircraft losses and low fuel. While awaiting Ghormley's reply, Fletcher repositioned his carriers which opened up Savo Island and Guadalcanal for Mikawa's approaching fleet.

In the meantime, Admiral Kelly Turner inadvertently received Fletcher's request to remove his carriers from the battle area. Turner's amphibious forces were still supporting the Marine landings and the offloading of supplies and munitions onto Guadalcanal. If Fletcher's carriers left the battle area, Turner's forces would be without air cover, forcing him to also withdraw his ships, and leaving the Marines to fend for themselves. This was another factor in the disaster that was soon to follow.

Faulty Deployment Around Savo Sound

Royal Navy Admiral Victor Crutchley, Amphibious Force Overall Commander, split his ships into three groups, each assigned to patrol an entrance to the anchorage off Savo Island. This patrolling formation resulted in three thinly spread forces unable to provide mutual support.

The Southern Group, commanded by Crutchley, protected Lunga Passage, the broad sweep of water between the north shore of Guadalcanal and the south shore of Savo Island. This group consisted of two Australian cruisers, HMAS *Australia* and *Canberra*, and USS *Chicago*, screened by the destroyers USS *Patterson* and *Bagley*. Crutchley selected a patrol pattern east to west due to heavy cross currents in his sector, which later proved to be a poor choice.

The Northern Group, commanded by Captain Riefkohl, was assigned to guard the approaches north of Savo Island, and consisted of the heavy cruisers USS *Vincennes*, *Quincy*, and *Astoria*, and the destroyers USS *Wilson* and *Helm*. Riefkohl chose a box-shaped patrol pattern, believing it to be the best chance to intercept ships coming their way.

Admiral Scott's Eastern Group, positioned in the opposite direction more than ten miles away from the Northern and Southern Groups, was not involved in the battle on August 9.

In addition to these three small groups of warships, the screening plan positioned two picket destroyers—USS *Ralph Talbot* and *Blue*—outside of Savo Sound. *Blue* was assigned patrol outside of Lunga Passage to "sound the alarm" for Southern Group, and *Ralph Talbot* patrolled outside the northern entrance for the Northern Group.

Crutchley's faulty deployment pattern around Savo Island greatly contributed to much of the confusion among the ships of the Northern and Southern groups. In the fight that would occur that night, communication between the Allied forces either failed or was non-existent. More than once Dad mentioned that "communications were poor back then."

Crutchley Removes HMAS Australia from Screening Groups

On the night of August 8, 1942, Admiral Richmond Turner summoned Marine General Alexander Vandegrift and Royal Navy Admiral Victor Alexander Crutchley to an emergency meeting onboard his Flagship *McCawley* to discuss Turner's dilemma due to Fletcher's decision to withdraw his carriers. Darkness and poor visibility prevented Crutchley from taking his floatplane to the meeting. Instead, he took the HMAS *Australia* to the rendezvous. This pulled Admiral Crutchley not only from his command of the defense force, but also took the HMAS *Australia* from the Southern Group at a most inopportune time, thereby reducing the Southern Group's combat power by a third.

Upon his departure, Crutchley left Captain Howard D. Bode of the USS *Chicago* in charge of the Southern Group, leaving the entire western line of defenses without overall tactical command. He also failed to notify Admiral Scott of the Eastern Group and Captain Riefkohl of the Northern Group of his ship's departure from the screening area. Captain Bode, thinking his commander would soon return from the meeting and unwilling to risk night maneuvering, decided not to place the *Chicago* as the flag in front of the *Canberra*. Failing to re-optimize the screening disposition, Bode retired for the evening without issuing night orders for the Southern Group.

Admiral Crutchley's meeting with Admiral Turner ended late evening of August 8, 1942. Due to the danger of rejoining the screening force at night under poor weather conditions, Crutchley decided to keep HMAS *Australia* with Turner's ships located several miles away from his screening forces. He failed to notify Bode of his decision to stay behind.

Just before midnight, *Vincennes* picked up a radio message from one of the destroyers. An unidentified aircraft had just been seen over Savo Island heading east toward the American ships. A lookout on the ship had also seen lights from an aircraft, but concluded the plane was friendly. However, Mikawa had sent last minute air reconnaissance of Savo Sound and now had intelligence on the deployment of his targets.

Crutchley's group endured two days of continuous GQ (General Quarters) and the ill-fated U.S. ships in the screening area reduced watch to "Condition Two" to allow much-needed rest for the weary crews. Riefkohl ordered his crew to be extra alert and ready for action, then retired to his cabin. While the captains of the Northern and Southern groups slept, Mikawa's large surface fleet was speeding down the slot toward his objective with his marauding ships in column formation.

Dad mentioned that the Americans expected the Japanese to attack at 8:00 the next morning.

CHAPTER NINE

DISASTER AT SAVO ISLAND

Around 1:45 a.m. on the fateful morning of August 9, 1942, Mikawa prepared for his attack in darkness. Approximately five miles away, the Japanese sighted the U.S. picket *Blue* heading directly toward them. Unaware enemy guns were now aimed at her, the *Blue* executed a pre-scheduled turn, and continued on with her patrol. USS *Ralph Talbot,* screening to the north, was oblivious to Mikawa's ships heading southeast toward the Sound.

With the aid of night binoculars, Japanese lookouts spotted the *Canberra* and *Chicago* in the Southern Group. Then Mikawa's men sighted the *Vincennes* leading the Northern Group as they proceeded southwest on the southern leg of their box patrol. Mikawa would have to engage two groups of warships before he could break through and attack the transports at Guadalcanal.

Battle of the "Sitting Ducks"

As the Imperial Japanese fleet entered Savo Sound, Mikawa selected his targets in detail. The enemy warships moved to the southern side of Savo, and Mikawa gave orders to fire torpedoes. Immediately, his lookouts sighted the destroyers USS *Bagley* and *Patterson,* leading the Southern Group, followed by the cruisers HMAS *Canberra* and USS *Chicago.* Mikawa's fleet began their independent firing.

USS *Patterson,* first to spot the enemy forces, frantically announced:

"WARNING—WARNING: STRANGE SHIPS

ENTERING HARBOR!"

As aircraft flares dropped overhead, directly above the *Canberra* and *Chicago,* only a few among Captain Bode's crew realized they were under attack. Torpedoes were reported approaching from starboard, and Captain Bode turned the *Chicago* in that direction, leading the ship to parallel the Japanese torpedo spread. Only moments later, her bridge lookouts sighted torpedoes to port, from *Chicago's* unengaged side. Bode swung his ship around again, trying to avoid the new spread, but in doing so exposed the entire length of the *Chicago* to the Japanese torpedoes.

Chicago took a torpedo and gun hit, causing slight damage, then sailed in the opposite direction of the attacking foe. Captain Bode had swung the crippled *Chicago* westward out of the fight. In the fog of battle, he had also failed to warn superiors and his other ships of the enemy's attack. The only contact made with the Southern Group was from Destroyer *Patterson*, who was battling with the Japanese cruisers, *Yubari* and *Tenryu*.

Shokai, Furataka, Aoba, and *Kako* then targeted the *Canberra,* who was taking torpedo hits to her starboard and port sides. The boiler rooms were knocked out, and the ship glided to a stop, completely out of commission. *Canberra* was out of the battle before her crew realized what had hit them. The Navy scuttled the Australian heavy cruiser the following day.

In the Northern Group, lookouts on the *Vincennes* spotted flares and star shells to their south, accompanied by a low rumble of gunfire. Assuming the flashes and flares of the battle were part of ground action on Guadalcanal, the crew on topside unknowingly watched Mikawa inflict a one-sided pounding on the HMAS *Canberra* of the Southern Group. Leaving the *Canberra* ablaze, Mikawa turned north for his second attack.

During the decimation of the Southern Group, the Japanese column formation began to break down. *Furutaka* suffered self-inflicted damage to her steering engines when she unleashed her main battery. At this point Mikawa's column inadvertently divided their single formation, with four ships on the right and three ships to the left in parallel fashion. To the right was *Chokai, Aoba, Kako* and *Kinugasa*. To the left were *Furutaka, Tenryu* and the *Yubari*. This worked to his advantage—*Vincennes, Quincy,* and *Astoria*, along with destroyers

Wilson and *Helm*, were now caught between the attack ships. Mikawa gave them a pounding.

The Japanese first sighted the *Astoria*. Lighting her with their searchlights, the *Chokai* opened fire with her guns and launched torpedoes. The *Astoria* returned salvos, but their confused Captain Greenman rushed onto the bridge ordering a cease-fire. The *Aoba*, *Furatuga*, and *Kako* immediately opened fire on the *Astoria* and launched torpedoes. Captain Greenman quickly reversed orders, but it was too late. The burning *Astoria* was left dead in the water and scuttled the next day.

The *Quincy* was the next target. Her Captain, Samuel Moore, struck by a shell en route to his station, left dying orders for the damaged ship to head toward Salvo Island and beach there. Suddenly, the *Farutaka, Tenryu*, and *Yubari* opened fire also. The *Quincy,* caught in the crossfire, sank bow first.

The gunners on the *Vincennes* had been constantly at their battle stations for two days; their energy was sapped from the muggy, tropical heat. E. J. Ridgeway had a sandwich in one hand and the other on his five-inch gun when the first melee broke out among the Southern Group. General Quarters called the crew to action. Soon every sailor manned his battle station.

Captain Riefkohl was awakened in his cabin, picked up his binoculars and rushed to the *Vincennes's* bridge, but was unable to determine the nature of the firing. The Captain ordered his ship to increase speed and waited for orders from Admiral Crutchley, but received no response. Concluding the shells now splashing around the

Vincennes were from friendly fire, the bewildered captain refused to shoot back.

Suddenly, the *Vincennes* shuddered—the Japanese had found range. Minutes later, a Japanese searchlight illuminated the heavy cruiser. Still convinced the firing was friendly, Riefkohl attempted to identify the *Vincennes*. He ordered the men to run up a large American Flag and illuminate the ship. Dad said, "We were lit up like a Christmas tree!"

Vincennes, now the primary target, was knocked back and forth as shells started slamming into her from port to starboard, and main battery fire struck her from stem to stern. Eight-inch armor-piercing shells continued to devastate the ship. Her bridge, carpenter shop, and radio antenna trunks were all hit. Finally, the ship's gunnery officer begged Riefkohl to give orders to return fire or they wouldn't have any guns left.

The words barely left his mouth when the ship's No. 1 and 2 turrets were knocked out of action from a direct hit. Still unconvinced as to the nature of the shooting, Riefkohl reluctantly gave the "open fire."

It was too late.

More shells began pounding the ship. Another torpedo hit No. 1 fire room, putting it out of action. More violent explosions followed, lifting the ship up out of the water and lurching her to starboard. She staggered momentarily and rolled to port. The list was heavy, and the *Vincennes* was settling fast. The men in the engine room were able to keep her engines going until the ship took another direct hit. Two "Long Lance" torpedoes blew an enormous hole in her No. 4 boiler

103

room. *Vincennes* jerked to a halt as her engine and boiler rooms began to flood, robbing her of all power. Totally defenseless, the ship remained under enemy fire until she was reduced to a flaming wreck.

Only twenty minutes into the battle, *Vincennes* was now dead in the water.

CHAPTER TEN

USS *VINCENNES* SINKS

Mercifully, around 2:20 a.m., Mikawa cancelled further strikes and retired from Savo Island at top speed to Rabaul, leaving the burning hulks of the *Astoria, Quincy, Vincennes,* and *Canberra* in his wake. In a little over 30 minutes, Admiral Mikawa's fleet sank four Allied heavy cruisers and killed more than 1,000 sailors at the Battle of Savo Island. Of the *Vincennes'* crew, 349 were killed in action, 292 were wounded, and over 800 survived. The *Quincy* had 300 dead and 167 wounded. The *Astoria* had 219 missing or killed. HMAS *Canberra* had 84 killed and 109 wounded.

As the *Vincennes* continued listing to port, Riefkohl issued orders to abandon ship. One junior officer, fresh out of the U.S. Naval Academy, was among the last of the crew to leave the ship. He later recounted that few men have stared into the face of such guns and lived—especially those stationed topside of the *Vincennes*.

Seaman Ridgeway was one of those on topside who survived. Knocked unconscious while supporting his five-inch gun, he finally came to, and found himself on the deck, surrounded by the charred bodies of his fighting companions killed in the attack. In the heat of battle, there was no time to grieve for the lost. He switched into survival mode. With a twisted leg, he limped into the waters and swam away from the sinking ship to avoid the whirlpool.

Chaplain Schwyhart was also among the last to abandon ship. He first assisted the wounded and helped them overboard. The chaplain walked into the water praying to God for help. Swimming furiously away from the sinking vessel, Schwyhart finally reached a fellow officer, looked back at the *Vincennes* and said, "Oh Chief, there goes our ship!"

Bobbing up and down in the shark-infested seas around Savo, the dazed and shocked survivors of the *Vincennes* watched their home sink into what would later be called the "Ironbottom Sound." The raging fires from their ship lit the waters crowded with men swimming toward life rafts or floating debris—anything they could hold onto. Flames from the still burning *Astoria* continued to illuminate the night sky at a distance until the ocean slowly extinguished the cruiser's fires, leaving them in total darkness. With so much blood in the water, sharks were now a threat.

Thousands of gallons of fuel from the sunken ships left a slimy, thick film over the waters of Savo Sound. Trapped in an oil slick that was burning their eyes and soaking their clothes, Ridgeway and his surviving shipmates held onto the hope of being rescued throughout that black night until the following morning when, at last, help arrived.

Joe Fritcher, GM/1c on the USS *Astoria*, gave the following account of his experience in the waters off Savo Island before being rescued:

> *"For our first two hours in the water, the battle raged on. We could hear gunfire and thought the Japanese were shooting survivors. Actually our destroyers were shooting sharks to keep them away from the men. While in the water, we were paddling toward land. But by the next morning, the tide had carried us at least 10 miles out to sea. A destroyer finally picked us up. I was so weak that I couldn't climb the sea ladder. They threw me a rope to put under my shoulders and then hoisted me up. It actually was a blessing that we didn't make it to land because we would have been captured."*

Finally, around 9:00 a.m., vessels were seen over the horizon, and the survivors wondered if they were friendly ships. It was an agonizing hour before they could see the destroyer USS *Mugford* slowly moving through the oil slick. The ship began her rescue of the weary, yet relieved men, struggling to keep afloat. Suddenly, *Mugford's* signal man announced they had picked up a submarine contact and would have to leave to drop depth charges. He instructed the survivors to keep their bodies, especially their abdomens, above water as much as possible to avoid underwater concussions. About an hour later, the *Mugford* returned and began the rescue by first collecting the wounded. By noon she had recovered around 400 men, mainly from the *Vincennes*.

By the afternoon of August 9, 1942, survivors from all three cruisers, including E. J. Ridgeway, were aboard the U.S. transport *Barnett* en route to Noumea, New Caledonia, along with some of the bodies recovered from the sunken ships. The dreaded task of "burying" the dead would be next.

Burial at Sea

The tradition of burial at sea is an ancient one and continues to be of extreme importance to the Navy brotherhood. To return to the sea is a noble symbol of the sailor's commitment to sea service. In preparation for burial, bodies were secured to a stretcher with a five-inch projectile placed between their legs, then wrapped in navy blankets with chains wound around them several times. The firing squad then signaled the pall bearers and bugler. The officer's call was next, "All hands bury the dead," as the ship came to a stop. The crew went into ceremonial formation and saluted.

Chaplain Schwyhart held a religious service with scripture reading, prayers, and a benediction. Three volleys were fired. As the bodies were draped with the American burial flag, the crew stood at attention while each hero was slipped into the sea from a special launching board. It was a gut-wrenching sight to see shipmates enter their watery graves.

The solemn burial ceremony was one of the few things E. J. Ridgeway shared freely about his war experience, probably because as a Church of God pastor after the war, funerals were an integral role of a minister.

On August 22, 1942, Seaman Ridgeway, along with other survivors, boarded the USS *Wharton* where they sailed to Samoa and then to Pearl Harbor, docking there on September 3. Upon arrival, everyone on the ship was detained. All the surviving officers from the three sunken U.S. cruisers were ordered for assembly. Soon, Admiral Nimitz arrived and informed the officers that the extent of the damage done at Savo Island on August 9 was still unknown to the Japanese. He warned the officers that these events were absolutely not to be discussed with anyone.

E. J. Ridgeway and the remaining survivors boarded the USS *Henderson*, bound for the States. They arrived at San Francisco on September 16, 1942.

The USS *Vincennes* would be awarded her second Battle Star posthumously, and Seaman Ridgeway would also be awarded Battle Star number two.

Internment on Treasure Island, San Francisco, California

The survivors of the *Vincennes, Quincy,* and *Astoria* experienced a rude awakening when they arrived at San Francisco. Adding insult to injury, they were placed under gag order and warned not to discuss the sinking of their ships to anyone. Instead of receiving a well-deserved hero's welcome, the surprised sailors were immediately interned on Treasure Island Naval Base and guarded as if they were prisoners of war.

When the family members of those killed or wounded at Savo Island received the dreaded knock of the Western Union delivery boy at their door, the telegram stressed that they keep secret the names of their loved one's ships that sank off Savo Island. The Axis press immediately released the American losses at Savo, but the disaster didn't hit American newsstands until mid-October 1942.

During this tumultuous time, President Roosevelt requested to extend the draft age to include males, ages 18 and 19.

My father never spoke about this experience, but a clue was given to me at his funeral by Lew Painter, my father's nephew, who was only a year younger than Dad. Lew had entered the Navy after he graduated high school. While on his ship, passing through the Treasure Island naval station, he spotted E.J. walking on a cane around the navy yard. Lew walked up to me after Dad's funeral service and angrily exclaimed, "They were treated like prisoners!"

At the time, I didn't understand what he meant, and looking back I wished I had pressed Lew for more details about this well-hidden episode of the war endured by the survivors of the *Vincennes, Quincy*, and *Astoria*.

During his time on the USS *Vincennes*, E. J. Ridgeway, only 20 years young, had sailed in the Atlantic and Indian Oceans, had crossed the Panama Canal, the Tropic of Capricorn, the Tropic of Cancer, the Arctic Circle, the Greenwich Prime Meridian, and the

110

International Dateline. He had participated in the Doolittle Raid and the Coral Sea Campaign, had fought in the battles at Midway and Guadalcanal, and had survived the sinking of the USS *Vincennes* off Salvo Island. Seaman Ridgeway was awarded two battles stars for Midway and Guadalcanal and seven certificates/citations.

Conclusion

Savo Island had been a major blow to the ego of the American military, who failed to anticipate the superior Japanese night fighting skills which in the end won the battle. Among the many important lessons learned from the tragedy was the need for the ability to fight at night. The U.S. Navy mastered the enemy's tactic and eventually turned it against them.

During E. J. Ridgeway's survivor leave and ultimate reassignment to the USS *Santa Fe* in October 1942, the following battles continued, leading to the final American takeover of Guadalcanal by February 1943:

- Battle of Cape Esperance – October 11 and 12, 1942
- Battle of Santa Cruz – October 25-27, 1942
- First Naval Battle of Guadalcanal – November 13, 1942
- Second Naval Battle of Guadalcanal – November 14, 1942
- Battle of Tassafaronga – November 30, 1942

New Commander of the South Pacific

The disaster at Savo Island and the defeat at the Battle of Cape Esperance caused Admiral Chester Nimitz to rethink his chain of command. He decided it was time for Admiral Ghormley to step down as Commander of the South Pacific and leader of the Guadalcanal Campaign. Nimitz determined that Admiral William "Bull" Halsey was the man for the job.

"Bull," as he was nicknamed by the press, was known throughout the Pacific for his fighting spirit. The day after Pearl Harbor, he had surveyed the damaged battleships and remarked, "Before we're through with them, the Japanese language will be spoken only in hell." Determined to take the fight to the enemy, Halsey led a series of raids against the Japanese in the Gilbert and Marshall Islands in February 1942. In April of 1942, he ushered the transport of Doolittle's bombers to within the hailing distance of Tokyo. His slogan was "Hit hard, hit fast, and hit often!"

As the newly appointed Commander of the South Pacific, "Bull" Halsey wasted no time in taking a hands-on approach that would finally bring the Guadalcanal Campaign to a close with an American victory. In a later quote, Halsey summed up the importance of the campaign, "Before Guadalcanal, the enemy advanced at his own pleasure. After Guadalcanal, he retreated at ours."

In early February 1943, the Japanese evacuated their remaining forces from Guadalcanal, conceding the hard fought campaign to the Allies. The Imperial Forces would have to change their battle stance from offensive to defensive as the momentum of the war in the Pacific had shifted to the ever-strengthening Allies, who were continuing to push up the slot toward Rabaul. However, the

Japanese high command vowed they would never again surrender an island to the Allies.

114

PART II

USS *SANTA FE* – CL 60

THE *"LUCKY LADY"*

CHAPTER ELEVEN

USS *SANTA FE* (CL-60)

Launched on June 10, 1942, USS *Santa Fe* (CL-60) was the fifth of the new Cleveland Class light cruisers designed by the U.S. Navy specifically for World War II with their increased cruising range, anti-aircraft armament, and torpedo protection. Miss Caroline Chavez of Santa Fe, New Mexico, sponsor of the ship, christened the vessel with water from the Santa Fe River, which had been blessed by the Archbishop of New Mexico's capital city. Beneath her mast were placed rare, vintage coins donated by the citizens of Santa Fe and the men of the New York Yard.

Later dubbed *"Lucky Lady,"* the light cruiser would see more action and receive fewer hits and casualties than any other ship in the

U.S. Navy. Involved in every major Pacific campaign from the Aleutians to the collapse of Japan, *Santa Fe* would receive 14 Battle Stars for her actions under fire.

Santa Fe's Gunnery Department

Because the ship is built for the gun, the largest and most important department on a warship is the Gunnery Department. Gunners Mates and their strikers had a huge task in the upkeep and maintenance of the various batteries—the booming six inch, the slamming five inch, the pounding forty millimeters, and the stuttering twenties. More than half of the men on the ship were in the Gunnery Department.

It was God's providence over E. J. Ridgeway, who had survived the sinking of the *Vincennes*, that his next ship assignment would be the "*Lucky Lady.*" By October 1942, he had earned the rank of Gunners Mate Third Class. With crossed cannons on his sleeve, E. J., along with 350 other veterans from the *Quincy, Vincennes,* and *Astoria,* became part of the crew of the USS *Santa Fe.*

Of the ship's full complement of 1200 plus men, the remaining balance were new recruits assembling later in November. At age 20, Ridgeway would now be considered an "old salt" among the *Santa Fe* crew.

Casablanca Conference

Just two months after the Allied landings in French North Africa in November 1941, President Franklin Roosevelt and British

Prime Minister Winston Churchill held a conference in Casablanca, Morocco to finalize Allied strategic plans against the Axis powers for the upcoming year (1943) and outline a policy for an unconditional surrender. Toward the close of the conference, the leaders agreed on a military strategy to stop Japanese aggression in the Pacific.

After the Casablanca Conference, the U.S. Seventh Naval Fleet formed to support General MacArthur's campaign in New Guinea. Admiral Halsey's Third Fleet in the South Pacific supported the Solomon Islands Campaign. Under Nimitz, Admiral Raymond Spruance commanded the Fifth Naval Fleet in the Central Pacific. E. J. Ridgeway and the crew of the *Santa Fe* would serve under Spruance's command for the next year.

USS *Santa Fe*, along with her "green recruits," left Philadelphia, January 11, 1943, on her shake-down cruise southward along the Atlantic Coast. After three days at Annapolis, the ship's Captain Berkey drilled his men in simulated battle conditions, fire control, and tested communication systems and engines. Ridgeway was assigned to the Gunnery Department, Third Division, whose crew would soon become proficient in manning mounts 51, 52, and 53 on the ship's quarterdeck as would be indicated by the *Santa Fe*'s scoreboard on her bridge.

On February 28, 1943, *Santa Fe* set sail from Philadelphia for the Pacific on a cold and snowy day. Passing down the Atlantic coastline through the Caribbean and Panama Canal, the ship conducted gunnery exercises throughout her voyage to Pearl Harbor. Entering the Hawaiian harbor March 23, 1943, the crew manned the rail. For most of them, it would be their first time to see the sunken *Arizona;* a sober reminder of the December 7, 1941 Japanese attack.

At Pearl Harbor, *Santa Fe* refueled and brought provisions aboard, including ammunition. During this time training exercises were conducted. Ridgeway and the other veteran crew taught the new recruits how to load the five-inch (55-lb) and the six-inch (134-lb) projectiles with their two-foot and four-foot powder cartridges. The six-inch projectile required three men for loading—one at each end lifting and then resting it on the middle man's shoulder to carry the heavy shell to the magazines below deck.

The *Santa Fe* was replenished and ready for her assignment in the impending Aleutian Islands Campaign—off mainland Alaska.

Operation Vengeance: Admiral Yamamoto's "Last Flight"

Prior to the Aleutian Islands Campaign, the U.S. Military engaged in "Operation Vengeance" with the intent to "take out" Japan's Naval Chief, Admiral Isoroku Yamamoto. On April 18, 1943, Yamamoto made his "last" flight. American cryptographers had broken a Japanese encrypted message revealing Yamamoto's flight schedule. U.S. long-range fighters intercepted his flight group and shot down his plane sending it crashing into the jungles of Bougainville. His body was recovered, cremated and the ashes taken to Japan by battleship.

Yamamoto's death was a quite a blow to the morale of the Japanese military, whose navy was now on the defensive, especially in the Solomons and the Aleutians. Conversely, it was a boost to the morale of the United States and the Allies as they had payback for his role in the attack on Pearl Harbor.

Aleutians Campaign: April 26 – August 15, 1943

With Japan's capture of Attu, Kiska, and Aggatu in the Aleutians in June 1942, a small Japanese force now occupied Attu and Kiska, posing an impending threat to the Northwestern United States. Designated to assist in routing the enemy from the Aleutians, *Santa Fe* set sail for the desolate island of Adak, April 15, 1943, for her first war assignment. She would be engaged in five arduous months of battling the harsh seas of these island chains near Alaska.

Some of the veterans on the *Santa Fe*—survivors of the sunken *Quincy*, *Astoria*, and *Vincennes*—made bets as to when their ship would go down as an attempt to intimidate the fresh sailors on board. Hoping to divert thoughts away from the dark humor, Ridgeway shared his previous experiences in Iceland and around the Arctic Circle. He advised the new recruits to be prepared for the rough, icy seas and freezing weather they were about to encounter.

Santa Fe left Hawaii on April 15 and five days later entered the icy channel of Kulak Bay. The ship faced the snow-covered mountains of Adak, Alaska, where U.S. forces had built facilities to retake Attu. The morning of April 21, 1943, the light cruiser headed west to report for duty with Cruiser Division 1, with the *Richmond* and *Detroit*, along with destroyers, labeled Task Group 16.6. The ships, covered with ice from stem to stern, moved on to Attu where they sortied without incident as they fought sudden violent squalls swooping out of the Bering Sea.

On April 26, the *Santa Fe* crew took their first shots in enemy-held territory—a shore bombardment of Attu. The action began when the beachhead was illuminated by a misfired star shell and a scare from a suspected Japanese reconnaissance floatplane that turned out to be a B-25 on patrol. The day climaxed when Task Group 16.6 unleashed a long-range bombardment on the Attu installations without any damage to the American ships from return fire. The group returned to Kulak Bay on April 28, 1943.

During the bombardment, Tokyo Rose had reported, "Attu was shelled by a battleship of the *Santa Fe* class."

Task Group 16.6 headed out on April 29 to resume reconnaissance of Attu's western approaches. While patrolling, *Santa Fe* had contact with one Japanese submarine on the 1st and 4th of May, but no action was taken. On May 11, the *"Lucky Lady"* became part of the covering force for the amphibious landings.

Attu Invasion

The American operation to retake Attu began on May 11, 1943. The *Santa Fe* and Task Force 16.6 closed in about 60 miles southwest of Attu Island to cover the troops as they waded ashore. Included with the invasion force were scouts recruited from Alaska, nicknamed "Castner's Cutthroats."

A shortage of landing craft, rocky, uneven beaches, and equipment inadequate for freezing weather hindered the Americans from securing beachheads on the island. Soldiers, not properly supplied with winter gear, suffered from frostbite and were unable to move their vehicles across the frozen terrain. Instead of a counterattack, the Japanese retreated to Attu's high ground in well-defended positions. U.S. military planners had thought this would be an easy mission, but icy weather, poor American logistics, and the fierce determination of the Japanese infantry proved them wrong.

The *Santa Fe* and her task force continued defending the seas off Attu blocking supplies and reinforcements to the Japanese until May 24 when she terminated her three-week patrol, joined Task Group 16.7, and returned to Adak, arriving May 26, 1943.

Meanwhile, U.S. ground forces scoured Attu Island, engaging in hand-to-hand confrontations as they searched for the dug-in enemy troops. The resulting fierce combat was costly—almost 4,000 U.S. casualties. With his soldiers starving and lacking ammunition, on May 29, 1943, Japanese Commander Yasuyo Yamasaki and his infantry charged wildly all the way into the rear of the American camp. The "banzai attack" ended on May 30, with a count of over 2,000 Japanese dead. Within two days, U.S. forces secured the island, and the Battle for Attu ended. It was the only land battle fought on American soil during World War II.

On May 29, 1943, *Santa Fe* got underway as part of Task Group 16.7, along with the *Wichita, San Francisco, Louisville* and four destroyers for patrol to the west. She remained in the patrol area until June 17, 1943, then joined Task Group 16.8 and departed for Adak. Between June 18-26, the task group conducted patrols of the island without incident.

On June 27, *Santa Fe* began patrolling the area north of Attu, again as part of Task Group 16.7. This task group included two battleships, three heavy cruisers, one light cruiser (the *Santa Fe)*, and seven destroyers. The ships fueled on July 3, 1943, and headed for the southern operation area via Amchitka Pass on July 4.

Kiska Bombardment

On July 6, the *Santa Fe* rejoined the three other light cruisers (*Wichita, Louisville,* and *San Francisco*), along with the two battleships (*Mississippi and Wisconsin),* headed for Kiska. The ships bombarded the fog-covered island, knocking out coastal battery defenses and making hits on anti-aircraft emplacements to prepare for the invasion. *Santa Fe* led the cruisers in column, and was the first to smother Kiska with her gunfire. There was no return fire from the Japanese.

Completing this assignment, *Santa Fe* returned to patrol the area south of Kiska and later headed for Adak. After replenishment, she rejoined Task Group 16.6, leaving Adak on July 20 headed for Kiska. On July 22, the group executed a second long-range bombardment using radar. With this mission completed, *Santa Fe* took patrol to the southwest to intercept a Japanese force reported to be approaching the Aleutian chain. No ships appeared, and *Santa Fe* steamed out of the operating area and headed back for Adak.

Battle of "Sitka Pip"

Upon completion of the Kiska bombardment, *Santa Fe* and her cruiser division patrolled to the southwest to intercept a strong Japanese cruiser-destroyer force reportedly approaching the Aleutian chain on the night of July 26. This turned out to be a laughable "snafu" later called the "Battle of Sitka Pip" among the veterans of the ships that participated.

Increasing fear, anticipation and excitement gripped the *Santa Fe* and her search party as their radar attempted to spot the approaching enemy that night. The captains of the ships frantically sent reports back and forth under code monikers such as "Crystal," "Joe," and "Cable" (*Santa Fe* was the "Lyric") to prevent disclosing their identities. Not long after midnight, one ship reported enemy contact on her radar screen. Almost simultaneously, several ships saw the same "pip" on their screens. It had to be the Japanese forces. All ships with radar contact were ordered to open fire. Every gun on every cruiser began firing, except the *Santa Fe*. The cool and calm Captain Berkey had ordered his ship to hold fire until she had a sure target.

The *Santa Fe* had one advantage over the vintage radar of her cruiser companions—she had been outfitted with the newest radar equipment operated by expertly trained personnel. Her radar specialists had correctly identified the radar pips on the screens of the other ships as "triple-trip echoes" from an island—Sitka—about 100 miles away. The firing from the other cruisers ceased only when they noticed that the "enemy pips" on their radar screen had not moved during the shelling. They had been shooting at ghosts.

According to official naval records, "The heavy ships of Task Group Gilbert punished the phantoms with 518 14-inch shells, 485 8-inch, 25 five-inch 38 caliber, and 76 five-inch 25 caliber."

Santa Fe, having held her fire, would later gloat over the other trigger-happy ships in the fleet's newsletter, with the following poem about "The Battle of Sitka Pip":

Hush my children! Button your lip,

And I'll tell you the Battle of Sitka Pip,

It all began in the early morn,

When Lava took his bugle and blew the horn,

Then Joe gave vent to his pent-up ire,

Pulled on his pants and opened fire

He was quickly followed by Lava and Cable,

Who pouted it out for all they were able,

At last, old Crystal with nothing to do,

Added her voice with a salvo or two,

Only Lyric, calm and serene,

Sat down on her duff with not a pip on her screen.

And so until morning with infinite care,

Lava, dear Lava, found pips everywhere,

At last came the sunrise a blessing so sweet,

So hush my dear children—please go to sleep.

Thus concluded the shadow fight at "The Battle of Sitka Pip."

Kiska Invasion

The next assignment of the *Santa Fe* was with Task Group 16.7, which left for Adak on August 3 and proceeded to the operating area north of Kiska. After a few days of uneventful patrol of that area, she returned to Adak, performing bombardment exercises for the next few days while the Kiska reoccupation force was assembling. On August 13, *Santa Fe* joined Task Unit 16.4, a gunfire support unit, and left Adak for the invasion of Kiska.

On August 15, 1943, a large invasion force of Canadian and American troops landed on Kiska while the *Santa Fe* and her group executed two bombardments in the Gertrude Cove area in dense fog with ship and fire control entirely by radar. The Allied ground forces found the island abandoned.

Under the cover of fog, the Japanese had successfully removed their troops on July 28. The Army Air Force had bombed abandoned positions for almost three weeks without suspecting the Japanese were no longer there. On August 19, the *Santa Fe* and her task unit left the area, arriving at Adak on August 20.

On August 25, 1943, the *Santa Fe* left Adak with her task unit en route to Pearl Harbor. Arrival at Hawaii on September 1, 1943, was just the refreshing change of environment the *Santa Fe* crew needed as a respite from their past five months of steaming some 48,000 miles and delivering four successful bombardments on the icy Aleutians.

USS *Santa Fe* earned her first Battle Star for her participation in the Aleutians Campaign. It would be Battle Star Number 3 for E. J. Ridgeway.

The crew basked in the balmy breezes of Waikiki beach and enjoyed the sites of the Hawaiian island. Cane fields, pineapples, papayas, surf boards, and hula shows were things to write home about. But the islands served more than just liberty ports—they provided the United States with a naval base, complete with dry docks, warehouses, and repair shops from which the American ships would sortie, attack, and retire back to Pearl Harbor.

The American offensive was increasing in the Pacific, and their primary naval base at Pearl Harbor was 3,520 miles from Tokyo. U.S. bases needed to be located closer to Japan, and Admiral Chester Nimitz had such a plan in mind.

CHAPTER TWELVE

NIMITZ ISLAND HOPPING STRATEGY

The Pacific Raids

While his fleet was building back strength from his losses at Guadalcanal, Admiral Nimitz planned to advance on Japan by seizing strategically selected islands, using each as a base for capturing the next. The campaign would begin in the Gilbert Islands, then the Marshalls, the Carolines, the Marianas, and Formosa. Once these islands were secured, the Americans would begin a full-scale invasion of the Japanese homeland. The starting point for this campaign was the small island of Betio on the west side of the Tarawa Atoll, located in the Gilberts.

Nimitz planned to send naval task forces on a series of minor raids prior to these invasions. The first would be a pre-invasion bombardment to soften up Betio Island. The second raid would be a diversionary attack on Wake Island to mask the upcoming invasion of Tarawa.

This would be the *Santa Fe*'s first in a series of engagements in the Pacific island-hopping strategy.

Tarawa Strike: September 11-17, 1943

At Pearl, *Santa Fe* joined the *Birmingham, Mobile,* and *Biloxi* to form Cruiser Division 13, under the command of Rear Admiral L. T. DuBose, who had shifted his flag from the *Birmingham* to the *Santa Fe*. On September 11, 1943, *Santa Fe* left Pearl Harbor as part of Task Force 15, for the air raid on Tarawa.

Santa Fe and her running mates, *Lexington* (newly commissioned)*, Princeton* and *Belleau Wood*, began a high-speed run on September 17, 1943, towards Tarawa Atoll and Betio Island in the Gilberts near the equator. Early the next day, all hands were at General Quarters watching the red and green lights of the planes of the first strike as they assembled over the formation. All morning, the planes flew bombing missions, destroying most of the Japanese aircraft on Betio's airstrip and doing a large amount of damage to enemy installations. With the assignment completed by mid-afternoon, the planes had returned to their carriers, and the group retired from the operation area.

Santa Fe returned unscarred to Pearl Harbor on September 23. Wake Island would be the next mission.

Wake Island Raid: October 5-6, 1943

Wake Island is an atoll consisting of three coral islets (Wilkes, Peale, and Wake) in the central Pacific Ocean about 2,000 miles west of Hawaii and 600 miles north of the Japanese-held Marshall Islands. Back in January 1941, American Naval planners had decided this atoll was the ideal site for an advance defensive outpost and began construction of military facilities there. However, eight hours after the Pearl Harbor attack, the Japanese struck Wake Island, and by December 23, 1941, they had seized the atoll.

At Pearl Harbor on September 25, 1943, Task Force 15 was disbanded and Task Force 14 (six carriers, along with two cruiser and five destroyer divisions) was formed for a diversionary attack to confuse the Japanese. On September 29, *Santa Fe*, part of Cruiser Division 13, proceeded with the carriers due west from Pearl Harbor for air and surface bombardments on Wake Island. On October 2, Task Force 14 split into two groups, with the *Santa Fe,* along with carriers *Belleau Wood, Essex*, and *Independence* in the northern section.

Early on October 5, 1943, Navy bombers swooped away from the flight decks to do their job on the Wake Island installations. Closing in from the north, the *Santa Fe* and her sister ships opened fire on the northern half of the V-shaped atoll. It was a two-way strike from both sea and air. Around the *Santa Fe*, the sea erupted with near misses from enemy artillery positions onshore. Twice, she evasively maneuvered in the waters during the land-sea duel.

131

On October 6, 1943, airstrikes on Wake were repeated and the following morning, the untouched ships cooled their guns and retired out of the fray. Black smoke spiraling on the horizon was a testament to the prowess of the *Santa Fe's* gun crew. The damage inflicted in the Tarawa and Wake Island raids was hardly crippling to the Japanese, but it gave the U.S. Navy experience for the greater campaigns to come.

USS *Santa Fe* had earned her second Battle Star. E. J. Ridgeway had earned his fourth.

Santa Fe Assigned to Fifth Fleet

Unchallenged during her five-day return trek, the United States fleet arrived at Pearl Harbor October 11. On October 13, 1943, Task Force 14 was promptly dissolved. Cruiser Division 13, with flagship *Santa Fe*, was assigned to Admiral Raymond Spruance for duty in the newly-created Central Pacific Force. Fifth Fleet was destined to carry the war from Pearl Harbor to the Philippine's in a year's time.

On October 21, 1943, as part of Task Group 53, *Santa Fe* sortied from Pearl Harbor en route to the Fiji-New Hebrides area for training prior to the occupation of the Gilbert Islands. Task Group 53 was the Southern Attack Force, assigned to take Tarawa, and *Santa Fe* was assigned to fire support with Task Unit 53.3. *Santa Fe* and her group proceeded southwest on November 2 to the west of Fiji and conducted training and tactical exercises.

Bougainville Operation: November 8-9, 1943

On November 3, 1943, the *Santa Fe* received an unexpected order to relieve battle-worn Cruiser Division 12, which had been supporting the Marine landing on Bougainville, the largest and northernmost of the Solomon Islands. Cruiser Division 13 and Destroyer Division 49 detached temporarily from Task Group 53 to operate with the naval forces under General Douglas MacArthur, Commander of the South West Pacific Area. Steaming at maximum speed and stopping only to refuel at Espiritu Santo, CruDiv 13 and DesDiv 49 anchored the next day at Tulagi's jungle-encompassed Purvis Bay on November 6, 1943.

Passing out of Tulagi through Ironbottom Sound, Ridgeway and other survivors of the *Vincennes, Quincy*, and *Astoria* stared grimly at the waters off Savo Island—the graveyard of their former ships that had been sunk August 9, 1942.

Rendezvous was made November 7, 1943, with a formation of reinforcements destined for Cape Torokina, a bulge on Bougainville's upper side adjacent to Empress Augusta Bay. There, the *Santa Fe* relieved the weary Cruiser Division 12 and took over the covering of reinforcements proceeding to Cape Torokina. Arriving at Bougainville near dawn, November 8, the four cruisers and accompanying destroyers steamed into an area about 25 miles to the west as the Marines landed on shore per schedule.

That evening, a low-flying enemy spy plane skirted the formation well out of the range of the AA batteries and gave the U.S. ships' location to every enemy south of Tokyo. After sunset, an estimated 30 to 35 Japanese twin engine planes swooped in from two directions, skip-bombing and torpedoing their way through a succession of fierce attacks. The rapid-firing cruisers retaliated, shooting down the enemy aircraft into the sea with as many as eight burning at the same time on the surface. *Santa Fe's* five-inch guns opened first, with Ridgeway at his turret, sending additional accurate fire at the Bettys now blazing into the sea, one after another. One flaming Betty passed over the *Santa Fe,* and her torpedo rack fell onto the main deck.

The cruisers, zigzagging at high speed, were difficult targets, but so were enemy torpedo planes making runs at 250 knots. Cruiser *Birmingham*, who had remained in the zigzagging formation in spite of one torpedo gash in her port bow and another in her stern, took another hit to her No. 3 turret but continued in action.

Two hours of intense fighting cost the enemy 15 of her finest torpedo planes. With her automatic fire power, the *Santa Fe* hit three planes, which were later painted on the ship. The surviving Japanese air fleet, with sightings now thrown off by the intermittent rain squalls and frustrated by the radical maneuvering and sharp shooting of Admiral Dubose's cruisers, quickly fled the area. The South Pacific Forces were able to secure a beachhead on Bougainville, on which airfields were constructed for the neutralization of the Japanese base at Rabaul.

On November 9, 1943, CruDiv13 and DesDiv 49 left with emptied transports and returned to and anchored at Purvis Bay the same day.

Tokyo Rose reported that Imperial Japan's Air force had taken a hit, losing 15 planes in the night action at Empress Augusta Bay, but then greatly embellished American losses: 3 battleships, 2 aircraft carriers, 7 cruisers, 13 destroyers, and an unknown number of transports.

Rear Admiral Thomas Browning Inglis, Commander of the damaged cruiser *Birmingham*, would later quip, "This would make *The Birmingham* a one-ocean Navy, for it was the only ship that's suffered a hit. Tokyo Rose is really a comedienne."

The Marines landed on Bougainville, and the special detail given to Cruiser Division 13 was completed, thus earning *Santa Fe* her third Battle Star and E. J. Ridgeway his fifth.

On November 12, 1943, *Santa Fe,* with her division and Destroyer Division 49, left Purvis Bay and steamed toward Espiritu Santo at high speed, arriving November 13. After refueling on the 14th, CruDiv13 was detached from the command of Admiral Halsey's Third Fleet.

On November 16, 1943, *Santa Fe* and her group, (now minus the *Birmingham* that was disabled at Bougainville), returned to the Gilberts and rejoined the huge amphibious Task Force 53 for the invasion of Tarawa. The cruisers and destroyers encountered no enemy opposition as they approached Betio Island the night of November 19.

CHAPTER THIRTEEN

BATTLE OF TARAWA

Gilbert Islands- November 20-23, 1943

Returning from Bougainville, *Santa Fe* rushed back to the Gilberts for the invasion of Tarawa—the first American offensive in the critical island-hopping campaign in the Central Pacific. The target was Betio Island, part of the Tarawa Atoll that included 15 other islands connected by sandbars, all surrounding a natural lagoon. Shaped like a narrow horn, the tiny island measured only 3,800 by 600 yards. The most fortified of any island invaded by the Americans during this campaign, it would be the first time that U.S. amphibious forces would face serious opposition from the enemy.

Japanese Defenses

The Japanese had worked for over a year constructing heavy, sophisticated defenses around Betio Island. The core of the defense consisted of two Japanese Special Naval Landing Forces (an elite corps of marine troops), supplemented by two Seabee-type construction units with a combined strength of around 4500 personnel, including some Korean conscripts. These personnel manned a massive defense system, consisting of a seawall made of logs from coconut trees three to four feet in height behind the beaches; a system of machine-gun positions behind the seawall covered with logs, sand, or an occasional armor plate of concrete and connected by trenches with rifle ports; 14 coastal defense guns with underground shelters for crews, fire control, and ammunition; 25 field artillery pieces in covered emplacements; 13-millimeter and 5-inch anti-aircraft guns; and 14 tanks with 37-mm guns. Personnel shelters constructed of concrete and coconut logs were connected at all points on the island. Betio's airstrip lay in the middle of the island and her beaches were strung with barbed wire and heavily mined. Confident their fortress was secure, the Japanese had been assured by Admiral Keiji Shibazaki that it would take a million men 100 years to take the island.

American Offensive Plan

Nimitz dispatched Admiral Raymond Spruance with the largest American fleet yet assembled for a single operation in the Pacific. Headed toward Betio were 17 aircraft carriers, 12 battleships, eight heavy cruisers, four light cruisers (including *Santa Fe*), 66 destroyers, and 36 transport ships. Aboard the transports were the Second Marine Division and a part of the Army's 27th Infantry Division, for a total of over 30,000 troops.

Gunfire planned for the support of the Marines, the heaviest bombardment executed up to this point in the war, was to be conducted in two phases. First, the heavy ships (four battleships and five cruisers), firing from positions off the beaches, would take out the coastal defense guns (which included four 8-inch Vickers purchased by the Japanese from the British in 1905) and organized beach positions. In the second phase, all ships (which included eight destroyers) would target the machine gun nests, rifle pits, and artillery positions along the beaches. After an intense 45 minutes of neutralization fire from the ships, all guns would be silenced to allow carrier aircraft to conduct strafing runs. Shore fire control parties with the infantry battalions would call for fire after the landing.

The invasion plan designated three major beaches along the northern coast of Betio as Red 1, Red 2, and Red 3. Red Beach 1 was on the far western end of the north side of the island. Green Beach, on the western shoreline, was planned for D-Day+1 landings.

Betio's airfield, running east to west, was bordered on the north by Tarawa lagoon and divided the island into north and south. Her west shore faced the deep waters of the Pacific, but the lagoon water was shallow. The Americans believed the beaches on the north shore provided a better initial landing location than those on the south where the water was deeper. The north shore on the island was bordered by a natural reef extending about 1200 yards offshore.

Initial concerns as to whether the landing craft could clear the reef had been dismissed as the military planners believed the tide would be high enough to allow them to cross. That assumption would prove deadly for the Marines landing on the island later the morning of D-Day. On this day and the next, the ocean experienced a neap tide (a tide of reduced range because the moon was near first or last quarter), and failed to rise the usual five feet above the reef.

The 76-Hour Battle

USS *Santa Fe,* assigned to Task Unit 53.3 as fire support to cover the landing of the Second Marine Division on Betio Island, patrolled close in-shore during the night of November 19, 1943, to prevent enemy planes from using the airfields. Shortly after midnight on D-Day (November 20), U.S. Task Force 53, escorting the Marine transports, arrived off Betio Island. During the early morning hours, errors in ship-to-shore movements of the transports resulted in a delay of H-Hour. Meanwhile, Japanese shore batteries opened fire on the transports before the U.S. ships could begin their planned bombardments of the island.

Santa Fe was patrolling the area southwest of Betio when the Marine transports came under fire. The light cruiser, along with Task Force 58, rushed to join the fleet heavies of Task Force 53 and pounded the island's coastal defenses. *Santa Fe*'s five- and six-inch guns drilled into thick, concrete bunkers for almost two hours, and three eight-inch batteries were knocked out. The bombardment temporarily lifted to allow the Marines to land.

Just before dawn, the first-wave Marines began approaching all designated beaches (1, 2 and 3) in their amphibious tractors (LVTs). The minesweepers began clearing the passage to Tarawa Lagoon around sunrise. A hail of fire from the Japanese coastal batteries greeted the U.S. ships, but the destroyers of Task Force 53 counter-attacked and silenced the enemy guns. American planes soon followed, bombing and strafing Japanese positions on the island.

The Alligator amphibious tractors successfully crossed the reefs, and the first-wave Marines landed on Red Beach 1 but were pinned down behind the seawall under heavy fire. Subsequent waves of Marines in landing craft (Higgins boats) began their approach toward all three designated beaches, but the operation soon encountered Betio's neap tide, now at a three-foot draft. The Higgins boats struggled among the reefs. The USS *Santa Fe* navigated the shallow waters of the lagoon and closed in for call fire in support of the stalled Marines. Forced to abandon the landing craft at the reef's edge, the Marines waded through waist-to-shoulder-deep water up to 700 yards under intense fire from the beaches' remaining, undamaged defenses. Many were cut to ribbons in the water.

The few men that made it ashore were exhausted or wounded. With essential gear soaked and radios useless, they were unable to communicate with their support units. The surviving infantry was now led by the guy next in charge, whether Lieutenant, Corporal, or Private. Finally, by midday of November 20, reinforcements had reached Red Beach 2. Colonel David Shupe collected his scattered men and ordered an attack. At day's end, about 5,000 Marines made it to Betio's shore, but the casualties were around 1,500.

As the sun set on Day 1, the anxious Marines waited through the long night, anticipating an attack in darkness. Unknown to the surviving soldiers was the fact that the Japanese Admiral and his officers on the island had shifted their command post to the ocean side of Green Beach and Red Beach 1.

During this move, the *Santa Fe* and her group closed to point blank range for call fire. The Japanese Admiral and his men had been spotted. One of the destroyer's five-inch shells exploded in their midst, killing the Admiral and most of his elite staff. The Japanese chain-of-command on the islands was broken.

The morning of Day 2, November 21, Japanese defenses had prohibited the Marines from moving inland to Betio's airstrip. In mid-battle, they redirected toward Green Beach on the western shoreline while Spruance's fleet bombarded the Japanese positions to prepare for the invasion. The enemy was silenced by precision gunfire from the American warships.

With support from infantry, tanks, and naval bombardments, the Marines attacked around 11:00 a.m., securing the beach within an hour. Around noon, by a seeming "Act of God," the tide suddenly came in and supplies and munitions were rushed to the Green beachhead. The secured beach allowed a fresh stream of infantry of about 1200 men to land and prepare to head eastward across the island. At 4:00 p.m., they reached the central runway, and by early evening of the second day, the Marines reached the southern shore, cutting the island in half.

On the morning of Day 3, November 22, the Americans began taking the remaining eastern and western ends of the airstrip, bringing in heavy tanks for support. By the end of the day they had pushed the remaining Japanese back to the eastern point of the airstrip. Late that evening, the Japanese regrouped for a counterattack and made a banzai charge into the teeth of heavy gunfire.

The morning of Day 4, November 23, the Marines had cleaned out all pockets of enemy resistance until less than 100 Japanese soldiers remained. The brave defenders continued their fight until desperation set in, and many performed seppuku rather than be captured. By noon, the Marines had reached the eastern tip of Tarawa, and the United States Flag now blew in the wind on the top of a palm tree on bloody Betio. The captured airfield would become their new central Pacific base at Tarawa allowing the Allies to continue their thrust through a much shorter route to Japan.

It had taken the Marines only 76 hours to take Tarawa—not 100 years.

Nearly 6,400 Japanese, Koreans, and Americans died on the tiny island in the 76 hours of fighting.

The *Santa Fe* had earned her fourth Battle Star and Ridgeway a sixth star for bloody Tarawa.

The cost of victory on Tarawa was high for the Marines who suffered 3,000 casualties. As a result, the naval and marine planners reexamined their amphibious warfare doctrine and concluded that neutralization of the beach defenses had been only a temporary solution that resulted in an excessive loss of American troops. Future operations would change in concept from neutralization to destruction, which could only be achieved by direct hits. This required slow and deliberate precision fire from the medium and heavy caliber guns at short ranges. E. J. Ridgeway's skill as a gunner would become more vital than ever in the future operations of the *"Lucky Lady."*

CHAPTER FOURTEEN

MARSHALL ISLANDS OPERATIONS
AND ASIATIC-PACIFIC RAIDS

Marshall Islands Operations

The next step in Nimitz's campaign in the Central Pacific Area was the Marshall Island chain, a key step in the island-hopping march to mainland Japan. About 2,500 miles southwest of Hawaii, the Marshall Islands were regarded by the Japanese as part of their "outer ring" of defense. At the end of World War I, these former German colonies were assigned to Japan as post-war settlements, and had since become an important part of both offensive and defensive plans of the Imperial Japanese Navy.

Once again, American intelligence had decoded Japanese radio traffic that detected the movement of Japanese troops to the outer Marshall Islands. Admiral Masashi Kobayashi, Regional Commander at Truk, had ordered battalions to Wotje, Maloelap, Jaluit, Mili and Majuro. Unknown to Kobayashi, the Americans would bypass these reinforced outer islands and invade Kwajalein and Eniwetok, the key atolls of the Marshalls.

Kwajalein Air Strike: December 4-5, 1943

In light of the heavy losses at Tarawa, U.S. military planners chose to employ both Navy ships and B-24 Liberators (heavy bombers) in a 15,000-ton pre-landing bombardment of Kwajalein—one of the most concentrated bombings to take place in the Pacific.

The *Santa Fe* left the Gilbert area with the Fifth Fleet and steamed north to launch carrier plane attacks on Kwajalein. Approaching the atoll from the north, the carriers launched their aircraft early morning of December 4, 1943. Throughout the day, Navy planes pounded Kwajalein and neighboring Wotje, snagging several anchored ships and a large number of land-based aircraft. The U.S. group retired shortly after sunset when the Imperial Air Force went into action.

With no opposition from American fighters, who had yet to master night-flight tactics, Japanese land-based planes swept in that night lighting up the task group with flares. Before the last attacks were repelled on early morning of December 5, the *Santa Fe* had opened fire twice without scoring any hits. Task Group 50.3 was free of damage, but the new carrier *Lexington* (CV-16), in nearby Task Group 50.2, took a torpedo hit aft, disabling her steering gear. Together, the two groups retired from the operational area.

Santa Fe had been underway almost constantly since October 13, 1943. Upon completion of the airstrike, the *"Lucky Lady"* welcomed orders to return to Pearl Harbor. The light cruiser arrived at Hawaii on December 11, 1943, and for the next two weeks received a work-over by the navy yard. More importantly, the ship became outfitted with more recently developed radar equipment. During that time, Captain Jerauld Wright replaced Captain Russell Berkey on the *Santa Fe*.

The Christmas mail bag arrived on board when the *Santa Fe* was ordered to the United States west coast to pick up the Kwajalein Invasion Convoy and escort them to Hawaii. On December 28, 1943, *Santa Fe* left Pearl Harbor for San Diego to report to Commander Group 3 of the Fifth Amphibious Force for training exercises prior to the Kwajalein Operation. On December 31, the destination changed to San Pedro, where the *Santa Fe* arrived on January 1, 1944. The new year would see the whole of the U.S. Navy in the Pacific on a full offensive move against Japan, whose naval power was on the decline.

Santa Fe joined Task Force 53 (Northern Attack Force) and spent two days in vigorous training exercises in the San Clemente area before returning to Long Beach on January 3. On January 13, 1944, *Santa Fe* left Long Beach as a unit of Task Force 53 for the invasion of Kwajalein and proceeded on to Lahaina Roads, Hawaii, holding daily training exercises en route. On January 22, Santa Fe departed Lahaina headed for the Marshall Islands.

Kwajalein Invasion: January 30, 1944- February 2, 1944

The United States assault on the bases at Kwajalein and Roi-Namur Islands, part of the Kwajalein Atoll, would be the first time the Americans penetrated the "outer ring" of the Japanese Pacific sphere. The American forces for the landings included two groups: Admiral Richmond Kelly Turner's Amphibious Force (Fifth Fleet) and Major General Holland M. Smith's V Amphibious Corp, consisting of the Fourth Marine Division (Major General Harry Schmidt), Seventh Infantry Division (Major General Charles H. Corlett), the 22nd Marines, and the 106th and 111th Infantry regiments.

The Sixth Japanese Base Force, under command of Rear Admiral Monzo Akiyama, headquartered on Kwajalein since August 1941, was the principal defense force of the islands. Akiyama's men spread out over a wide area, with IJN air bases located on Roi-Namur, Mili, Maloelap, Eniwetok, and Wotje. The defense system on the islands was mostly in line, with little or no depth. The 22nd Air Flotilla, depleted after the Gilbert campaign, had less than 150 aircraft remaining in the Marshalls.

On January 29, 1944, the *Santa Fe* detached from Task Force 53 and led a "maverick" group for bombardments on Wotje. Beginning at dawn January 30, the ships went into formation firing on the coastal batteries, the two airstrips, buildings, and installations on the island. Fires were started in several areas and all targets assigned were well covered. The *Santa Fe* ceased firing early that morning. All ships completed their runs before 2:00 p.m., and the group rejoined Task Force 53 for the approach on Kwajalein.

The Wotje attack was part of the plan to catch the Japanese off guard. It was evident that the well-equipped outer shell of the Marshall Islands would be costly to capture. By simply feinting then side-stepping and moving on to the more vulnerable center atoll of Kwajalein for control of the air and sea lanes of the mid-Pacific, the attack would appear to the Japanese as the usual American pre-invasion bombardment.

On January 31, 1944, Task Force 53 arrived off Roi-Namur Island before dawn to cover the approach and entry of American landing craft into the Kwajalein Atoll. *Santa Fe's* Captain Wright directed the heavy guns toward Roi, which was supported by four coastal defense guns, 28 anti-aircraft guns, four blockhouses, and 17 pillboxes with machine guns. Around 8:45 a.m., shells from the support ships reduced all beach defenses on the southern and western perimeter of the island in preparation for the landing scheduled the following day. Several blockhouses and batteries were knocked out. Around 3:00 p.m., firing completed for the day, and the *Santa Fe* retired with the transports for the night.

As H-Hour approached on February 1, the support ships closed in on Roi-Namur and delivered another heavy bombardment on the southern beaches. The landing craft lined up and headed inward. The nearer the ships approached the beach, the more intense came their barrage. When the boats were nearly beached, a spotting plane circling overhead dropped a cluster of signal flares, and *Santa Fe* and her ships redirected their shells further inland, enabling the Marines to advance behind the curtain of fire.

By nightfall, occupation of the island was assured. Three days of preliminary bombardment at Roi-Namur proved the worth of the new doctrine of destruction versus neutralization. Japanese defenses were almost completely obliterated, and U.S. casualties were only a small fraction of those suffered at Tarawa. From now on, precision destructive fires from the heavy ships were features of the preliminary assaults in forthcoming amphibious operations.

On February 2, 1944, *Santa Fe* was in the Roi Island anchorage, and the following day left the support at Roi for her next call of battle—the impregnable Truk in the Carolines. At dusk on February 6, the light cruiser navigated through the narrow channel into the newly-seized Majuro Atoll to join Task Force 58. Arriving at Majuro on February 6, she was assigned to Task Group 58.1. Majuro became her base of operations, bringing the *Santa Fe*'s engagement in the second step of the Central Pacific campaign to a close.

While Betio's airfield in the Gilberts had been vital for long-range bombers, the importance of the Marshall Islands became altogether different. Consisting of three atolls, Majuro, Kwajalein, and Eniwetok, with lagoons that could harbor large numbers of ships, the Marshall Islands were now staging points for future operations. Also, they would be the genesis for Admiral Nimitz's "secret weapon." With two of the three atolls captured—Kwajalein and Majuro—Pearl Harbor would no longer be the westernmost U.S. Naval port of call.

In the twin attacks on Kwajalein and Roi-Namur, the Japanese casualties numbered almost 8,000. The U.S. Marines suffered less than 2,000.

Santa Fe now had five Battle Stars to her credit, and E. J. Ridgeway had seven Battle Stars under his belt.

To ensure air and naval superiority for the upcoming invasion of the last major Japanese base in the Marshalls (Eniwetok), Admiral Raymond Spruance dispatched Task Force 58 for strikes on Truk in the Carolines.

Asiatic-Pacific Raids: February 16 – May 1, 1944

Truk Raid: February 16-17, 1944

Japan had invaded and occupied the Caroline Islands during World War I, and after the war, received a League of Nations mandate over both the Marshall and Caroline Islands. During the 1920's and '30's, in violation of this mandate, the Japanese shut off the Carolines to the outside world, and began building airstrips and fortifying key islands, especially Truk's main islands. By the time Japan launched their attack on Pearl Harbor, she had four military airstrips, extensive fortifications, and major naval installations at Truk. By July 1942, the island had become the main base for the Imperial Japanese Navy's Combined Fleet, and beginning in late August 1942, Admiral Isoroku Yamamoto, Commander-in-Chief of the Combined Fleet, had located his headquarters on the battleship *Yamoto* in Truk Lagoon.

Fast Carrier Task Force

During World War II, the first large-scale use of aircraft carriers took the place of the battleship force as the primary striking arm of the United States Pacific Fleet. The flat-deck carriers, utilized as portable airports, embarked aircraft which were brought to the battle by the "flattops." This enabled U.S. naval forces to project air power great distances without having to depend on local bases for staging operations.

Admiral Marc A. Mitscher, of Doolittle Fame, was primarily responsible for developing the operational tactics of the newly formed Fast Carrier Task Force. At this point in the Pacific war, the U.S. carriers inflicted considerable damage on the Japanese naval forces in a series of quick air strikes. Under Mitscher's direction, U.S. naval air power would enter a new realm wherein the carriers could challenge enemy land-based planes over more sustained periods of time. This attack force would participate in all the Navy's battles in the Pacific during the last two years of the war, and the *Santa Fe* would be among the support ships.

The Fast Carrier Task Force, consisting of several task groups, was normally built around three to four aircraft carriers, screening destroyers, cruisers, and the newly built fast battleships. The task groups operated independently or combined with the others as the battles dictated. Strikes against island strong points were undertaken by one or two task groups, but when a major operation was underway, the task force utilized all four groups together.

By early February 1944, Admiral Mitscher's Task Force 58 was assigned to attack Truk, the "Gibraltar of the Pacific." The goal was to eliminate a possible Japanese threat from that base against the American operations in the Marshall Islands.

Mitscher's formidable Task Force 58 consisted of five fleet carriers (*Enterprise, Yorktown, Essex, Intrepid,* and *Bunker Hill*) and four light carriers (*Belleau Wood, Cabot, Monterey, and Cowpens*), embarking more than 500 planes. An impressive fleet of seven battleships and numerous cruisers (including the *Santa Fe*), destroyers, subs, and other ships supported the carriers. With the invasion and bombardment of the Marshalls behind them, Task Force 58 left Majuro for an airstrike on the Truk fortress.

Santa Fe's next excursions would be the heart of the cruiser's battles. At this point, the ship began establishing her role among TF 58 as a fast-attack cruiser, striking the Japanese unexpectedly and quickly moving to the next target, thereby creating an illusion of several attack groups.

From her new base at Majuro, on February 12, 1944, *Santa Fe* sortied with Task Force 58 across 500 miles of enemy waters toward the Truk bastion of strength. After fueling at sea on the 14th, the next day was a high speed run toward the target. On February 16, the task force came in behind a weather front, surprising and catching the Japanese off-guard, and launched six airstrikes unopposed. Mitscher's group retreated the area, leaving behind many ruined ships and scores of destroyed planes.

Around 9 o'clock that night, the enemy began their first intense air attack and raids soon followed. The tropic moonlight was

153

etched with tracer patterns as the American ships beat off low-level torpedo attacks until 2:00 the following morning. The only ship damaged was the USS *Intrepid* in an adjacent task group.

On February 17, the Americans continued their strikes until noon. The total score for this one raid at Truk was over 250 Japanese planes destroyed and 18 of Japan's ships, including two cruisers, sunk. The Americans lost only 17 planes. After the strike, the U.S. forces bypassed Truk, her supply lines now disrupted.

Saipan Raid: February 21-22, 1944

Retiring toward the Marshalls, the task force refueled, and on February 20, 1944, changed course toward Saipan (the crown jewel of Nippon's outer defense chain) in the Mariana Islands. At dusk on February 21, a Betty was shot down as it sneaked away. The task force knew it would have to fight its way to the target.

Just after dark, the battle started. All night the enemy land-based planes went down in flames, ignited by American bullets. The *Santa Fe* destroyed one Betty heading directly toward her. A dive bombing attack by Vals broke up with no damage to U.S. ships. The air fight continued until noon February 22, and in its aftermath, the carriers launched scheduled airstrikes for the rest of the day.

The American ships returned to the Marshalls and anchored in Majuro on February 26, 1944, no longer having to return to Pearl Harbor for replenishment. During this operation, *Santa Fe* completed 100,000 engine miles.

Emirau Invasion: March 20, 1944

One week later, *Santa Fe* detached from Admiral Spruance's Fifth Fleet and steamed to Espiritu Santo to join Admiral Halsey's 38.1 Task Group. On March 17, 1944, Halsey's force covered the occupation of Emirau Island, the last of a series of engagements comprising "Operation Cartwheel," MacArthur's strategy to surround the major Japanese base at Rabaul. On March 20, a force of nearly 4,000 Marines landed on the unoccupied island, where an airbase was soon to be developed, forming the final link in the chain of American occupied bases around Rabaul.

On March 27, *Santa Fe* rejoined Spruance's Task Force 58 for the next operation at the Western Carolines.

Palau, Yap, and Woleai Raids: March 29 – April 1, 1944

USS *Santa Fe* was once again a member of Spruance's Fifth Fleet fast carrier task force headed for the Palau Islands in the Western Carolines. Southeast of Palau, on March 29, 1944, Japanese torpedo planes attacked from sunset until late evening, and several planes were put out of action by U.S. guns. No American ships suffered damaged. On March 30, U.S. carriers launched the first strikes against the Palau Islands, inflicting heavy damage on that enemy base. Upon final recovery that evening, *Santa Fe* along with Task Group 58.1, steamed toward Yap to launch more strikes and beat off a heavy, five-hour attack that night.

On March 31, Navy planes blasted Yap and the following day, pounded Woleai with no enemy opposition. During the three-day campaign, over 100 Japanese planes were destroyed in combat and more than 40 on the ground. As a result, MacArthur's New Guinea campaign was able to move forward without threat from the Western Carolines. *Santa Fe* and her Task Group 58.1 retired to the southeast and returned to Majuro on April 6, 1944.

In the Marshalls, Kwajalein, Majuro, and Eniwetok were the prototypes for the advanced supply, repair, and fueling stations Nimitz had envisioned as "secret weapons" essential to the Pacific Campaign. With these bases established, Wotje Island would now be the *Santa Fe* crew's respite while their ship was being refueled and replenished.

During this time, MacArthur had scratched his way through the mountains of eastern New Guinea and became anxious as the fight labored on at a slow pace. While MacArthur's army advanced only from Australia to Rabaul, Admiral Nimitz steamed through the Gilberts, Marshalls, and Carolines and was about to use the Pacific Ocean as a highway to strike the Marianas and Formosa, bypassing the Philippines en route to Japan. MacArthur's troops would now have to slug their way through western New Guinea toward his ultimate destination, the Philippines, and he was not about to let the Navy steal the show. He had earlier declared to the Filipinos, "I shall return," and he intended to do so in person.

Finally, Washington, D.C. relented to political pressure from MacArthur, and ordered Nimitz to cover the Army's invasion of Hollandia. On April 13, 1944, the *Santa Fe* left from Majuro, with Task Force 58, and proceeded southwest toward New Guinea to assist MacArthur's SouWesPac.

Western New Guinea Operations: Support for Hollandia Invasion

Wadke and Sawar Airfield Bombardment – April 21-22, 1944

Hollandia Island had a good potential harbor and three airstrips capable of rehabilitation and enlargement. On April 21, 1944, the day before the landings, the Navy's carriers launched airstrikes over Hollandia, including Wadke and Sawar airfields, 150 miles to the west of the island. That night, the *Santa Fe*, with Cruiser Division 13 and Destroyer Division 91, temporarily dispatched from the carrier group and bombarded the air installations on Wadke and Sawar Islands.

Early morning of April 22, 1944, the *Santa Fe* and company opened fire and sent over 10,000 rounds of five and six-inch "calling cards" into the installations on these islands. The bombardment operated entirely by radar as the island's installations were not visible from the ships. Reports from observation planes the following day confirmed their firing had been on target. Completing the operation around 2:00 a.m., the group resumed normal stations with their carrier force Task Group 58.1.

At dawn, April 22, the amphibious landing took place and MacArthur's forces made their first big jump, moving from Saidor 500 miles along the north coast of New Guinea and landing at Hollandia and Aitape.

Truk and Ponape Strikes: April 29- May 1, 1944

With strikes on Hollandia completed, on April 26, 1944, *Santa Fe* with Task Force 58 headed east to the vicinity of Manus Island, just north of Papau, New Guinea, for refueling and aircraft replacements. On the evening of April 28, the task force took a northerly course headed for the Truk fortress. After crossing the International Date Line on the "second" 29th of April, Task Force 58 launched airstrikes on Truk. With another significant line crossing under his belt, Ridgeway was now considered a "Golden Shellback."

Strikes were repeated on the 30th and then additional strikes were launched against Satawan. Several enemy alerts came during the day, but none of their planes attacked the force. On May 1, 1944, the carriers proceeded eastward hitting Ponape with airstrikes and surface bombardments on the way to Kwajalein and anchored there on May 4.

Santa Fe received her sixth and seventh Battle Stars for her participation in the Asiatic Pacific Raids and the previous Hollandia Invasion. Ridgeway received his eighth and ninth Battle Stars.

"Make all preparations for making port!" was always a welcome change from the rigors of battle. The plan of the day included repairs, paint, and provisions for the ships of Task Force 58 now anchored on Kwajalein. Rust spots were covered with yellow chromite, and crewmen loaded ammunition by the fantail crane from dawn to dusk.

Sailors had one break each day. Every afternoon, an LCI (Landing Craft Infantry) took 300 men to shore to swim, play ball, catch a few uninterrupted rays of sun, and consume their allotted three beers. Those who didn't drink would always give their brewskies away, resulting in a few "drunken sailors" returning to the ship. Play days ended soon enough, and the crew of the *Santa Fe* knew that orders were just around the corner to set the special sea detail.

The *Santa Fe* remained at Kwajalein until May 13, 1944, on which date she proceeded to Majuro, anchoring there for the remainder of the month. Intense anti-aircraft practices were conducted, and on May 29, *Santa Fe,* with Cruiser Division 13, was at sea for two additional days of target practice of all types in preparation for more heated action to come.

CHAPTER FIFTEEN

MARIANAS OPERATIONS AND
FIRST BATTLE OF THE PHILIPPINE SEA

Marianas Operation: June 11 – August 5, 1944

Saipan, Tinian, and Guam Strikes: June 11-15, 1944

The Marianas, consisting of an almost continuous chain of islands extending 1,350 miles southward of Tokyo, were considered important for several reasons. According to Admiral Ernest J. King, Chief of Naval Operations, the Marianas were strategic to the western North Pacific because they dominated the sea and air lines of communications with Japan's Inner South Seas Empire. Capture of the islands would provide the U.S. Pacific Fleet with bases from which they could attack these lines of communication and strike Palau, the Philippines, and Formosa and then bomb Tokyo and other Japanese home islands.

Saipan, the key to the Japanese defenses, was the first target. Having been in Japanese hands since World War I, the island's fortifications were formidable. Saipan was surrounded by a coral reef, and the U.S. Navy knew it would be an extremely difficult landing. Surface ships would conduct a heavy bombardment two days prior to the invasion scheduled for June 15.

The fast carrier task force of Fifth Fleet, under Admiral Marc Mitscher, prepared the way for the assault. On June 6, 1944, the same date of the D-Day invasion of Normandy, Task Force 58 (now composed of 4 carrier task groups) left Majuro. The first two days were spent in rigorous training exercises with Task Group 58.7, a surface striking force, after which the *Santa Fe* joined Task Group 58.2.

On the afternoon of June 11, TG 58.2 launched their first strike against land-based aircraft and air facilities in the Marianas. Daily airstrikes continued against Saipan, Tinian, and Guam, blasting Bettys and Zekes on their runways to soften enemy defenses.

On June 15, Japanese torpedo planes came in for the attack. According to Dad, these Bettys zeroed in on the ships flying in at such low levels you could see the pilots' faces. Instead of targeting the plane, he shot into the water in front of the nose of the aircraft hoping for one of two results. The explosion would either spray water over the windshield to blind the flyer's view, or create a column of water that would be like a concrete wall should the plane fly into it. The gunners from the U.S. ships smothered the attackers with AA fire allowing the Marines to begin establishing their beachhead at Saipan.

Leap-frogging Across the Pacific

Up to this point, the U.S. Navy had moved across the Pacific, seizing one island base after another. Strategically, not every Japanese stronghold had to be captured; some, like the big bases at Truk and Rabaul, were neutralized by air attack and then simply leapfrogged. The goal was to get close to the Japanese mainland and then launch massive strategic air attacks leading up to an all-out invasion.

The "Decisive Battle" Theory

Alfred Thayer Mahan (1840-1914), one of the giants of naval military thought, wrote extensively on naval strategy and the history of sea power. His lectures, beginning in 1885, at the newly established Naval War College (of which he eventually became president), were the basis for his most important work, *The Influence of Sea Power Upon History: 1660-1783*, published in 1890. Mahan's philosophies dominated global naval thought from the early 1900's to the late 1930's, and especially influenced Imperial Japanese Naval doctrine during World War II, although Yamamoto's decisions to divide his battle fleet was a deviation from the theory. With the advent of carrier air power, Mahan's influence waned among the U.S. Naval planners during the Pacific War.

Mahan had asserted that the primary mission of a battle fleet was to engage the enemy's fleet in a clear-cut victory which became known as the "decisive battle." At Saipan, the Japanese Imperial Navy, as Mahanian doctrine suggested, intended to draw the American ships away from their covering position of the invasion/landing forces into the Philippine Sea for such a decisive battle.

First Battle of the Philippine Sea: June 19-20, 1944

The "First" Battle of the Philippine Sea in June 1944, took place during the American amphibious invasion of the Mariana Islands. It was the last great "carrier-versus-carrier" duel between the American and Japanese naval forces, involving the U.S. Navy's Fifth Fleet, as well as ships and land-based aircraft from the Imperial Japanese Navy's Mobile Fleet and nearby island garrisons. The victory would give the United States control of the seas enabling the Marines to secure Guam, Saipan and Tinian Islands that provided air bases within range of B-29 bombers targeting Japan. The engagement was entirely an air battle, in which the Americans had all the technological advantages.

To keep Saipan out of American hands, Japan's only defense was to eliminate Spruance's Fifth Fleet. On June 16, Vice Admiral Jisaburo Ozawa steamed out of San Bernardino Strait with his mobile strike force, comprised of ninety percent of the Japanese Fleet. The force was led by nine carriers, including the newly armored-deck *Taiho,* with 473 planes, 18 battleships and cruisers, and 28 destroyers—about half the size of the American force. Ozawa's inexperienced and poorly trained pilots were fiercely proud, but were outnumbered 2-1.

164

Ozawa's Strategy

Ozawa's carrier planes were lightly armored enabling them to fly greater distances while the American carrier planes, with heavier protection for their pilots, had less range. Consequently, Ozawa determined to position his ships beyond the striking range of the U.S. planes, while allowing his aircraft to be within striking distance of the American fleet. After attacking the carriers, the enemy could refuel at Guam for a return strike en route to their carriers. Ozawa also counted heavily on the 500 or so ground-based planes that had flown ahead to Guam and other islands in the area.

Spruance's Strategy

Admiral Spruance's primary goal was to protect the landing/invasion forces at Saipan, but he knew that the Japanese fleet now posed a genuine threat to the operation. Spruance detached Task Force 58, with Admiral Mitscher in command, and kept the escort carriers behind to protect the invasion forces. Mitscher moved out in a defensive formation with 15 carriers and 956 planes, plus 28 battleships and cruisers, 69 destroyers, and 28 submarines. This set the stage for the "decisive battle" that Ozawa, using Mahan's theory, had anticipated.

The Battle

The Americans spotted Ozawa's scouts on the afternoon of June 18—both forces were now aware of their opponent's location. Ozawa resisted the impulse to attack immediately knowing his planes would have to land that evening, which would force his inexperienced pilots to land in the dark.

Mitscher's fleet was right where he anticipated. It seemed Ozawa's plan had worked to perfection on paper, but the repeated raids on Guam and the surrounding islands had destroyed many of his land-based planes and airfields.

The Marianas Turkey Shoot – June 19, 1944

The attack began on June 19, 1944, with Ozawa's first wave of 64 planes. From Pearl Harbor, Admiral Nimitz instructed Spruance's carriers to utilize their radar in intercepting Japanese communications. This enabled the combat information centers to radio the American fighters, allowing them to intercept the enemy 50 miles out. Between the Hellcats and the U.S. surface ships, 42 Japanese planes were shot down. One Japanese bomber registered a hit on the battleship *South Dakota*, with no serious damage to ship, but inflicting 50 casualties.

Some planes of the second wave managed to attack Task Group 58.2, protected by the *Santa Fe,* and had near misses on the *Wasp* and *Bunker Hill*. Two more waves were launched and suffered heavy losses, including attacks on the airfields where Ozawa's planes had planned landings. Out of 373 planes launched from Ozawa's carriers, 243 were shot down, with about 30 others severely damaged. Including the strikes on land bases, the Americans had destroyed almost 300 enemy aircraft, with the loss of 17 Hellcats and eight bombers in a single day.

During a debriefing after the first two air battles, a pilot from the USS Lexington remarked, "Why, hell, it was just like an old-time turkey shoot down home!" Afterward, the first day's battle of the Philippine Sea would be referred to as "The Marianas Turkey Shoot."

Although no U.S. planes had registered hits on the Japanese fleet, two U.S. submarines attacked their carriers. The *Albacore*, struck the new Japanese fleet carrier *Taiho*, and by 3:30 the afternoon of June 19, Ozawa had transferred his flag to a cruiser, as the *Taiho* sank. Almost simultaneously, the *Cavalla* sent a spread of six torpedoes with three hits on the *Shokaku*, a veteran of Coral Sea. She sank three hours later.

Day Two

By June 20, as Ozawa's fleet retreated toward Japan, American scouts located his ships approximately 300 miles distant and just out of round-trip range. With the knowledge that his pilots might not make the return flight before evening, Mitscher launched 230 torpedo planes and dive bombers. Sighting the Japanese Mobile Force, the American planes sank the light carrier *Hiyo*, and damaged the carriers *Chiyoda*, *Junyo*, and *Zuikaku*, the battleship *Haruna*, and several Japanese planes. On that black, moonless night, American pilots with no landing experience began returning to darkened flattops. Many ditched in the water.

The *Santa Fe* and her running mates turned on every available light and fired star shells, but plane casualties were still high. The destroyers cut rapidly to the point where the planes' running lights had disappeared into the sea and as a result, a great majority of the flight crews were saved. Low on fuel, the ships turned eastward on June 21, 1944. Air support at Saipan had been taken over by the "baby" carriers, and, after fueling, *Santa Fe* and her Task Group 58.2 headed toward Eniwetok for replenishment. On June 24, the carriers launched a small attack on Pagan Island, hitting the airfield there and then proceeded back to Eniwetok.

The Americans lost 130 planes and 76 men in one of the greatest victories in world naval history. Japan lost 450 planes, three carriers, and 445 of its best remaining pilots. Admiral Spruance's forces inflicted heavy damage on Japanese surface ships and successfully prevented further enemy interference to U.S. operations at Saipan.

The Marianas-Saipan Land Battle: June 15 – July 7, 1944

On June 13, 1944, American battleships began a two-day pre-invasion bombardment of the north and south shore of Saipan. The island was an important Japanese commercial port including its Aslito Airfield.

In preparation for an invasion, the Japanese placed target flags in the bay to measure their cannon fire. D-Day was June 15, and the Second and Fourth Marines and 27th Army Infantry began their invasion on the west shore with 300 landing craft. The beaches were lined with barbed wire, mines, and machine guns; nevertheless, the U.S. occupation forces secured the beachhead by nightfall.

The Japanese, with a larger force inland, dug in on the high ground along the mountainous terrain of Mount Tapochau. At nightfall, the Japanese attacked, taking heavy losses, but the U.S. Marine's beachhead held. The following day, supporting infantry landed, and the Marines pushed toward Aslito Airfield. Once again, the enemy attacked after dark but were finally repulsed. Japanese fighting men hid in their caves by day and were hit hard by artillery, machine guns, flame-throwers, and fire-shooting tanks.

On July 7, 1944, a desperate banzai charge was led by virtually every enemy survivor left on Saipan—approximately 3,000 men—some on crutches, some bandaged, and some carrying bamboo swords. Adding to the horrors, Japanese civilians on the island had believed propaganda that death was preferable to the torture they would be subjected to by their American captors. As a result, they threw themselves and their children off the cliffs of Saipan into the sea. Almost 30,000 Japanese soldiers died or committed suicide, including the disgraced Admiral Chuichi Nagumo.

Honolulu Conference

On July 4, 1944, a semi-secret conference was held at Pearl Harbor between President Roosevelt, Army General MacArthur, and Naval Admiral Nimitz to negotiate their differences for the final strategy to defeat Japan.

The Army and Navy had been at loggerheads regarding future operations. Admiral Ernest J. King and other members of the Joint Chiefs of Staff, had favored blockading Japanese forces in the Philippines and attacking Formosa to give the Allies control of the sea routes between Japan and southern Asia. General Douglas MacArthur favored an invasion of the Philippines, which also lay across the supply lines to Japan. Leaving the Philippines in Japanese hands would be a blow to American prestige and a personal affront to General MacArthur. The result of the Honolulu Conference was "Operation Stalemate II," a plan which dictated that Nimitz support MacArthur in taking Peleiu Island, freeing the Army General to move on to the Philippines with naval support.

The Japanese received hints of America's decision to invade the Philippines almost as soon as MacArthur, Nimitz, and Roosevelt adjourned their conference at Pearl Harbor. Imperial Japan's combined fleet could no longer launch a general offensive against the now overwhelming American superiority. Japan's air power had dwindled to a meager force of land-based planes operating from the Philippines, Formosa and the Bonins, and most of the Japanese surface ships were based in the southwest off Singapore. However, the aircraft carriers had to be based in Japan to reform their air groups.

Japanese control of the Pacific Ocean became greatly diminished with the capture of the Solomons, the Gilberts, the Marshalls, the Carolines, the Marianas, and New Guinea. Only the screen of islands from the Japanese homeland through the Ryukyus, Formosa and the Philippines protected the rich flow of oil and other strategic supplies that were the lifeblood of Japan's war effort. The southwestern area, the main source of Japan's materials, was heavily fortified—so was the island chain, linking the area to the Japanese homeland.

The Japanese commanders still hoped they might have a chance against the powerful oncoming U.S fleet. The Imperial High

Command would have to concentrate all its available forces for one last massive counter-blow. The attack had to be perfectly synchronized allowing their limited forces to take their best shot.

The result was the Japanese Sho-Go (Victory Operation) Plan devised in four distinct versions, depending on where the Americans would make their next major thrust. Sho-1 was for the defense of the Philippines; Sho-2 would defend Formosa, the Ryukus and the southern Japanese home islands; Sho-3 would be used to defend central Japan; Sho-4 would defend the Kuriles in the north.

With the American plan to invade the Philippines now confirmed at the Honolulu Conference, Nimitz would continue his island-hopping, but with an emphasis on Iwo Jima and Okinawa.

Iwo Jima Bombardment, Pagan Island Strikes, Guam Strikes/Invasion: July 4-21, 1944

USS *Santa Fe* returned with her fleet to Eniwetok. On June 30, 1944, she as a unit of Task Group 58.2 headed for the enemy air base at Iwo Jima, which was their first point of attack. Around noon on July 3, the CAP shot down a Japanese scout plane. The task force believed they had now been sighted by the Japanese. As the American ships closed in toward Iwo Jima, that afternoon a fighter sweep launched to prevent enemy air attacks that evening.

On the Fourth of July, the *Santa Fe*, along with her forces, gave the island a special fireworks display, shelling Iwo Jima with direct fire at ranges between 9,000 and 16,000 yards. The tremendous amount of firepower destroyed the airfield, but the bombardment failed to penetrate into the caves of Mount Suribachi.

On July 5, the carriers launched a small airstrike on Pagan Island and then passed south striking Guam and Rota. Japanese planes approached the formation during the evenings of July 7 and 11, but were shot down by night fighters. On July 14, the operation area was moved west of Guam, and strikes continued until July 21, 1944, the day of the Guam landing.

Strikes on Yap and Ulithi: July 25-28, 1944

On July 22, 1944, Task Groups 58.1, 58.2 and 58.3 moved further south, and on the afternoon of July 25th launched daily strikes against Yap and Ulithi, with no enemy return fire. Operations were completed on July 28, and that evening the fast striking task groups departed for the Marianas arriving off Saipan on August 1. *Santa Fe* anchored briefly at Saipan for refueling on August 2, 1944 and then proceeded underway with her task group en route to the Bonin Islands.

Bonin Islands Strikes: August 4, 1944

The Bonin Islands, only 500 miles off the coast of mainland Japan, consisted of about 30 islands, the largest of which are Iwo Jima and Chichi Jima. Iwo Jima had two airfields holding 80 fighter aircraft. Chichi Jima had a large enemy garrison, a good harbor with a substantial naval base, but no beaches suitable for landings. During this action, the American strikers encountered fierce fighting by some of the finest land-based Japanese pilots, equipped with the latest fighter aircraft.

After fueling on August 2, the *Santa Fe* and her task group followed a northward course en route to the Bonin Islands for airstrikes and bombardments, with the first sweep scheduled for August 4. Around 8:00 a.m., search planes reported a Japanese convoy leaving Chichi Jima. Carrier Task Group 58.1 was ordered to locate the convoy and make it a primary target. Planes launched at 9:30 a.m. and at 11:30 a.m., reported an attack on the enemy ships.

Early that afternoon, Cruiser Division 13 and Destroyer Division 91 detached from the task group to zero in on the enemy convoy and proceeded to pass between Ototo and Yome Jima. The destroyers sighted and sank a small craft.

Radar targets picked up two enemy ships to the northwest; one was identified as a destroyer. That night, the *Santa Fe* and accompanying cruisers fired on the ship. Return fire was light. Destroyer Division 100 received orders to finish off the target, but the Japanese destroyer sank on its own.

Chichi Jima Bombardment: August 5, 1944

The American cruisers headed northwest and closed in on another target. En route, the *Santa Fe* fired on and left burning a large enemy landing barge, while the other cruisers finished it off. The ships turned southward toward Chichi Jima. Shortly, enemy planes were detected approaching, but their air attacks were uncoordinated and driven off by the *Santa Fe* and her task group.

Enemy attacks from the air eventually ceased, and the ships formed into a bombardment disposition and fired on shipping in the harbor of Futamiko at Chichi Jima. Three runs were made under return

173

fire from a heavy enemy battery that was finally silenced, and the U.S. fleets escaped damage. After the bombardment was completed, several enemy ships were sunk, the seaplane base damaged, and fires were left in their wake. The *Santa Fe*, along with her force, rejoined the task group to the southeast of Chichi Jima.

The evening of August 5, the *Santa Fe,* with Cruiser Division 13, detached from the carrier group and proceeded south. On August 7, these ships joined Task Group 58.7, which was composed of surface ships only. Training exercises were held during the next three days.

On August 11, *Santa Fe* anchored at Eniwetok, having completed a cruise of 42 days, during which time the ship steamed 17,656 miles, an average of 420 miles daily.

"Lucky Lady" now had eight Battle Stars and Ridgeway had ten.

Navy "Two Platoon System"

By August 1944, Admiral Spruance's Fifth Fleet numbered 16 carriers, six battleships, and 80 cruisers and destroyers. The job of leading this huge armada was too much for one admiral to manage for the duration of the war. Therefore, the Navy developed the "two platoon system," where every six months, the two senior admirals, Spruance and Halsey, switched off as commander of the fleet. Whenever the admirals changed command, so did their fleet's name and number designation. When Admiral Spruance's Fifth Fleet was in operation, Admiral Marc Mitscher served as the tactical commander of Task Force 58. When the fast carrier force rotated to Admiral

Halsey's Third Fleet, Admiral John S. McCain, Sr. was in tactical command and the ships were designated Task Force 38. Mitscher served as commander of Task Force 38 under Halsey until McCain became acclimated to the task.

Planning for upcoming operations was completed whenever Spruance and Halsey rotated out of active command. This rotation in command enabled the U.S. Navy to perform at a higher level, while at the same time intimidating the Japanese with the appearance of greater U.S. naval assets than were actually available. When Admiral Spruance turned over command of his Fifth Fleet on August 26, 1944, it became Halsey's Third Fleet.

Personality-wise, the difference between Spruance and Halsey was day and night. Spruance, nicknamed the "electric brain," was known for his intellect, quiet and reserved manner, and calculated tactics. Spruance was a favorite among the admirals. "Bull" Halsey on the other hand, was loud, impulsive, and egotistical, but also determined and very popular among the sailors. As a "brown-shoe admiral," Halsey, a naval aviator, had somewhat of an edge over the "black-shoe admiral" Spruance, a naval surface warrior with no aviation experience. The yeomen of Spruance's Fifth Fleet were excited when Halsey took over, but also anxiously curious as to where the "Bull" would charge next.

CHAPTER SIXTEEN

WESTERN CAROLINE ISLANDS OPERATIONS

Palau (Peleliu), Mindanao, East Leyte, Manila, Luzon, East Samar: September 6 – September 24, 1944

After the capture of the Marianas, Admiral Nimitz's forces moved to the west and south to attack the Western Caroline Islands. Establishment of U.S. forces there would give the Americans control of the southern half of the crescent shaped chain of islands that run from Tokyo to the southern Philippines. Nearly 800 ships participated in the operation.

U.S. Pacific forces centered their attention on the Japanese-controlled Island of Peleliu, viewed as a potential threat to General

MacArthur's posed invasion of the Philippines. Peleliu's airfield would enable Japanese planes to strike at the planned American landing and support ships and menace their troops once on the ground. The assault on Peleliu would have the highest casualty rate of any amphibious invasion, in terms of men and materials, in the entire Pacific War.

Santa Fe was assigned to Task Group 38.3, under the Command of Rear Admiral Frederick Sherman on the *Essex.* This fleet, with two similar carrier groups, completed Task Force 38 under command of Admiral Marc Mitscher on the *Lexington.*

On August 30, 1944, *Santa Fe*, with her task group, sortied from Eniwetok as part of the Surface Striking Force for training purposes. On September 3, all ships rejoined the carrier groups. After gunnery exercises they joined with Third Fleet Commander, Admiral "Bull" Halsey, whose flag was on the *New Jersey,* and launched strikes on the Palau Islands, September 6 and 7, 1944.

Mindanao and Bislig Bay Action: September 9, 1944

On September 9, U.S. carrier planes sighted and attacked an enemy convoy of about 40 ships on their first sweeps over Mindanao Island, the second largest and southernmost island of the Philippines. Pilots reported at least 20 remaining Japanese ships running for cover in Bislig and Hinatuan Bays on Mindanao. The cruisers *Santa Fe* and *Birmingham*, along with Destroyer Division 110, were ordered to finish off the enemy convoy.

At first, the cruisers and destroyers passed back and forth across the mouths of the two bays, pumping shells into the convoy. As they entered the bays at close range, all their gunners cut loose. The lightly armored Japanese vessels attempted to fire back but were met by overwhelming gunfire from the American ships. Expending 1,789 rounds of six-inch, five-inch, and 40mm ammunition, the *Santa Fe* sank 4 of the 15 ships she raked during the two-hour battle. The gunners did their usual superb jobs on these shoots, and the remaining ships were left behind burning or severely damaged.

Santa Fe left Bislig Bay and rejoined Task Group 38.3. Airstrikes against Mindanao were resumed on September 10, 1944, and the following day, the task group headed east to fuel. The lack of opposition at Mindanao prompted airstrikes into the central Philippines. From September 12-14, the American ships launched airstrikes against the Visayan area (the central islands of the Philippines) while standing off Dinagat Island.

A Japanese bomber penetrated the task force screen on September 13 and scored a near-miss on the *Langley*, while the *Santa Fe* fired and drove off the lone enemy plane. On the 14[th,] the cruiser's two seaplanes teamed to rescue two downed aviators, and that evening the ships departed the area.

Santa Fe's Task Group 38.3 then went to the support of the U.S. Marine assault on Peleliu Island. Like Saipan, the Japanese prepared Peleliu and its airstrip in anticipation of an American invasion. This time, however, their defensive strategy changed. Instead of meeting their attackers at the beaches, as they did at Tarawa, the Japanese planned to disrupt the landings by fortifying Peleliu's unique terrain. The wide coral reef was strung with barbed wire, and ammunition shells with exposed fuses were planted underwater. Only a limited number of their fighting men manned the machine gun nests as their first line of defense. The majority were stationed inland in caves just above the invading U.S. forces so as to inflict the maximum amount of damage on the troops below. The inner island defenses were constructed in Mount Umurbrogol, which had hundreds of honeycombed limestone caves, interlocked and protected by slanted, sliding steel doors with heavily fortified bunkers surrounding them. The airstrip was located on the south end of the island.

On September 15, around 8:30 a.m., the First, Fifth, and Seventh Marines attacked from the southwest toward Peleliu's airfield. While the coral reefs did not hinder the landing craft, the Japanese defenses on the island took their toll. More than 50 of the landing craft were taken out, but by 9:30 a.m., Marines landed on shore establishing a beachhead. The enemy continued to attack but were repulsed and by nightfall, Marines were ashore with about a thousand casualties.

However, there remained one major obstacle—the Japanese had not exposed their inner defenses. Marine commanders mistakenly believed that the enemy line would crumble the next day.

Peleliu, the "Forgotten Battle": September 16-18, 1944

This operation took place in a forgotten backwater of the western Pacific where marines, soldiers, and sailors fought one of the bloodiest battles against the Japanese in World War II. The assault on the Island of Peleliu, planned as a supporting attack for MacArthur's return to the Philippines, qualifies as one of the most fabled battles in American History in terms of ferocity and valor.

From September 16-18, 1944, USS *Santa Fe* and her forces operated westward of Palau in readiness to provide air support for the landing operations on Peleliu Island.

On the 16[th,] the Marines moved across the airfield as enemy guns from Mount Umurbrogol fired down upon them. By nightfall, the Peleliu airfield, which was the primary objective of the entire operation, had been captured. The Americans used the island's airfield on the third day of the invasion and began dropping napalm on the steel doors to the entrance of the caves. The Marines headed north toward the island's Mount Umurbrogol. They engaged in fierce hand-to-hand combat, with the American flame-throwing tanks clearing out most of the caves. When the battle ended, it would be known as the bitterest battle of the war for the U.S. Marines.

Combined, both Marines and Army suffered 1,800 killed in action and some 8,000 wounded. The Japanese had over 10,000 killed and 200 captured. Almost two and a half years later, on April 22, 1947, a Japanese Admiral finally convinced a lieutenant and 33 men still hiding in the caves of Peleliu Island that the war was over.

The all-out Allied offensive was underway to gain and maintain the eastern approaches to the Philippines–Formosa–China coastal areas.

Manila Raids, First Phase of the Philippine Campaign: September 21-24, 1944

On September 21, 1944, Ultihi, an atoll of the Peleliu Islands consisting of 34 islets, was seized by the Americans with no resistance from the Japanese. With a natural lagoon larger than Pearl Harbor, it could anchor more than 700 ships. Admiral Nimitz's secret weapon had been realized. Within a month, floating dry docks were established for repairs of vessels of all sizes and purposes. One victual ship baked fresh bread and pies, another distilled water, and one even made over 500 gallons of ice cream a day. The island of Mog Mog became famous for rest and recreation for the U.S. sailors, marines, and soldiers.

With Peleliu Island firmly in American hands, U.S. carriers stood by to provide air support as an American Naval unit steamed northwest toward Luzon to launch its first airstrikes on Manila scheduled for September 21 and 22, 1944. On the 24th, the Visayan area was again the target, and continuous airstrikes were launched on the Central Philippines from an area off San Bernardino Strait.

Santa Fe received her ninth Battle Star, and Ridgeway received Battle Star number 11.

After the first phase of the Philippine Campaign was over, the *Santa Fe* anchored in Kossol Passage, Palau Islands on September 27. Due to insecurity of the open reef surrounding the anchorage and the possibility of night air and surface attack from Japanese forces on Babelthuap (only five miles away), *Santa Fe* sortied nightly while at

Kossol, returning in the morning for replenishing. On October 1, the task force proceeded to Ulithi, Caroline Atoll, which was developing into the forward base of future U.S. fleet operations.

In September of 1944, American airstrikes against the Philippines during the Peleliu occupation was proof that carrier-based air power could successfully attack large areas protected by enemy land-based planes and also could protect itself against counter blows. As a result, Admiral Halsey recommended to Nimitz that strikes on Luzon to the north or Mindanao to the south be cancelled, and that U.S. forces concentrate on Leyte with its gulf as the next target. With a population of over 900,000, Leyte could be expected to assist an American invasion, since many of its residents had already supported the guerrilla struggle against the Japanese in spite of harsh repression.

The Joint Chiefs of Staff and General MacArthur supported Halsey's recommendation and moved up the initial date for the Leyte landings from December 20 to October 20. In preparation, the Navy's Third Fleet conducted strikes on enemy installations in the Philippines, Formosa, and Ryukyus.

Philippine Liberation: October 10 – 20, 1944

Okinawa and Formosa Strikes: October 10-13, 1944

The *"Lucky Lady"* sortied from Ulithi, October 6, with Task Group 38.3, to conduct fast airstrikes in preparation for landings in the Philippines. The intent was to keep the enemy guessing where the American forces would land next. Proceeding northwest on October 10, Santa Fe and her unit moved into position south of Okinawa and bombarded the airfields and shipping facilities. While the Japanese were still reeling from this blow, the action quickly shifted to Formosa and Pescadores, which were hit heavily on October 12, 1944. These strikes on aviation facilities, factory warehouses, wharves and coastal shipping, had been anticipated by the Japanese. For the first time in this series of operations, a large number of enemy land-based planes were over the targets and anti-aircraft fire was intense.

Late that evening, the Japanese made their first counterattack. Night torpedo bombers made run after run, only to burst into orange flames as anti-aircraft fire hit home with coordinated attacks from various directions, aided by the use of flares. Emergency maneuvers and stack smoke were used to avoid enemy return fire. The last American planes were returning to their carriers at sunset when enemy planes again closed in for a night attack. The Japanese were quickly repelled by gunfire. When attacks finally ceased around 2:30 a.m., Task Group 38.3 had escaped unharmed. In spite of opposition, 193 enemy planes were shot down and 123 more destroyed on the ground.

On Friday the 13th of October 1944, the carrier planes were back over Formosa, and the enemy air force lashed out in full fury when the task force withdrew at nightfall. Combined gunfire from the "Lucky Lady" and her cohorts turned back the Japanese air forces, but around 6:30 p.m., the unlucky heavy cruiser USS *Canberra* in Task Group 38.1 took a torpedo in her engineering spaces. Needing a tow, Cruiser Division 13 detached to assist the *Canberra*, thus forming

Task Group 30.3, composed of the *Santa Fe, Birmingham, Mobile*, and six destroyers.

Task Group 30.3 headed out to escort and protect the stricken *Canberra* which was being towed at a mere 4 knots. The group was 120 miles from Formosa and within range of enemy aircraft on Okinawa, Luzon, and Formosa. Daylight air attacks were completely repulsed, and the *Santa Fe* kept the *Canberra* covered with stack smoke, while adding one more enemy plane to her total. The Japanese targeted the slow moving convoy, but were repelled by the *Lucky Lady*, who was soon supported by more destroyers and the light carrier USS *Cabot* and later USS *Cowpens.*

On October 14, *Houston,* having replaced the stricken *Canberra,* and her escorts encountered another heavy air raid. *Houston's* gunners shot down three of the attacking torpedo bombers, but a fourth torpedo hit her engine room, and she now required a tow. Captain Behrens and his damage control crew managed to keep the *Houston* afloat and slowly continued toward Ulithi. In order to prevent further air attacks while the damaged ships retired, the carriers launched repeated fighter sweeps and strikes over Formosa and northern Luzon on October 14 and 15.

By October 16, both the *Houston* and *Canberra* were under tow to Ulithi for repairs. That afternoon, another Japanese plane, still determined to sink the *Houston*, struck her stern, flooding her scout planes' hangar. All of her surplus sailors evacuated to escorting ships. Captain Behrens of the *Houston* transferred a couple hundred of his ship's survivors to the *Santa Fe*. Several Marines who came onboard begged Captain Wright to let them man one of the gun mounts to exact

185

revenge on the Japanese, should they attempt another attack on the *Houston*. Wright assigned them to a gun position on the *Santa Fe's* bow.

Halsey's Bait Force

That night, Tokyo Rose gave the American admirals an idea after her announcement of the "annihilation" of the Third Fleet as a victory for Imperial Japan. She reported that 20 American carriers had been sunk along with numerous support ships. Realizing the Japanese had mistaken the injured *Canberra, Houston* and her escorts as the remnants of Task Force 38, Halsey conceived the idea of using the "crippled" cruisers as a bait force to set the stage for the enemy's propaganda. He would lure the Japanese air corps and surface ships into a surprise attack on the two stricken cruisers, all the while thinking they were finishing off the Third Fleet.

Halsey's gamble was disturbingly dangerous, leaving the *Santa Fe* and her fellow guardians as open targets while they screened the slow-moving *Houston* and *Canberra*. CruDiv 13 and its charges continued toward distant Ulithi while Task Force 38 moved off to lie in wait. Then *Santa Fe* began to send out clear radio messages indicating their location, inviting a Japanese attack.

The enemy took the bait and sent out her battleships and cruisers to finish off the Third Fleet. Unfortunately, a reconnaissance plane discovered the genuine Third Fleet, who was waiting to spring the trap, and the IJN retreated without firing a shot. However, Japanese land-based planes continued their pursuit of "Cripple

Division 1." They attacked in waves, hoping that a few might make it through the CAP to finish off the damaged cruisers and their escorts.

Tension mounted on the *Santa Fe*. The jittery nerves of the weary crew kept them on edge as the alarm from general quarters sounded throughout the day and night. Ridgeway and the entire gunnery division remained on duty at their stations, straining their sleep-deprived eyes in an attempt to detect the enemy planes from the Americans.

That afternoon, one Japanese plane slipped through the CAP, and evading the AA fire, headed straight for the *Santa Fe*. Suddenly, the enemy plane changed trajectory and let loose a torpedo striking near the *Houston's* stern and exploding into a ball of flame. Seconds later, another bomber headed straight for the *Santa Fe's* starboard side. Every gun on the ship was firing into the plane, but she kept coming. The torpedo dropped, then the plane attempted a suicide dive.

The bow of the cruiser was now hidden by the flames and black clouds that surrounded her. Observers from her companion ships felt the *Santa Fe* had run out of luck. Known for getting out of trouble as quickly as she got into it, the *"Lucky Lady"* emerged from the smoke and fire unharmed. Due to the skillful maneuvering of Captain Wright, the ship's stern was turned toward the approaching bomb so that the waters from the wall of the wake caused by the churning propellers detonated the warhead.

Still, the crew on the *Santa Fe* was not without casualties. The bomber had struck the water close to ship's forecastle, splashing flaming fuel over the 20mm guns that were manned by the Marines from the *Houston* and several others of the ship's crew, as well as

Marines who were observing nearby. A half dozen men were engulfed in flames. The guns of the *Santa Fe* and her fleet continued firing on the approaching enemy planes trying to finish off their job. Thankfully, no more planes made it through the screen.

Medical attention was given to the wounded. (Ridgeway later recalled to a fellow pastor having held his best buddy's right arm, while the ship's surgeon cut off the left one and threw it into the sea.) When the skies cleared of all danger at sunset, *Santa Fe's* crew participated in a burial at sea for one of the marines who had died from his burns.

On October 17, 1944, the weary *Santa Fe* detached from the screening unit of the *Canberra* and *Houston* and returned to Task Group 38.3 the morning of October 18. The next few days, TG 38.3 operated about 300 miles east of Luzon as a supporting force for the landings on Leyte Island scheduled for October 20. The amphibious forces of the Navy's Seventh Fleet were in support of MacArthur's infantry, but he now expected additional support from Halsey's Third Fleet carriers to the north of the landings for defense against the Japanese on both land and sea.

Japanese Victory Plan for the Philippines

The Japanese received their first solid evidence of America's plan to invade the Philippines in the middle of October 1944 when Mitscher's mighty Task Force 38 closed within 50 miles of Formosa and launched airstrikes for MacArthur's invasion. The IJN immediately put their Philippine defense strategy, Sho-1, into action.

188

The risky plan dictated that their four fleets, separated by thousands of miles of ocean, synchronize their movements with impeccable precision.

From Japan's inland sea, the surface ships would sortie to attack, and if everything went according to the plan, the land-based aircraft would assault the American carrier groups, while a decoy carrier group, led by Vice Admiral Jisaburo Ozawa, lured Halsey's Third Fleet north away from San Bernardino Strait. Exploiting the gap created by Ozawa's diversion, a battleship force under Vice Admiral Takeo Kurita, would sneak into the waters off Samar, through the San Bernardino Strait, and then south to Leyte. Another force, under Vice Admiral Shoji Nishimura, with Vice Admiral Kiyohide Shima's Third Section in support, would sail through the Surigao Strait.

Bearing down on MacArthur's landing beach from the north and south, the two Japanese battleship forces planned to catch the American troops in a pincer movement. The heavy ships would sink, at will, any U.S. transports and supply ships off Leyte, then turn their guns inland to blast the American Army from the rear while Imperial troops rushed ashore. The plan required impeccable timing, but if successful, the Japanese could surprise and scatter MacArthur's troops then escape before Halsey diverted his ships for a return air strike.

Visayan Invasion Support: October 20, 1944

October 20, 1944 was D-Day for MacArthur's leap to the Philippines. That same day, *Santa Fe*, with Task Group 38.3, headed northwest, and the carriers launched two strikes over the Visayan and Sibuyan Sea area returning eastward that night.

USS *Santa Fe* was awarded her tenth Battle Star, and Ridgeway received Battle Star 12.

CHAPTER SEVENTEEN

BATTLE OF LEYTE GULF
(AKA: SECOND BATTLE OF THE PHILIPPINE SEA)

The Battle of Leyte Gulf is generally regarded as the largest naval battle of World War II. The battle, initially named by the Navy as the Second Battle of the Philippine Sea, was later changed by military historians to the Battle of Leyte Gulf most probably to emphasize the Army's role. In naval lore, it will always be the Second Battle of the Philippine Sea. Up until this time, the brunt of the Pacific battles had been borne by the navy and marines while MacArthur's army struggled in Australia and New Guinea. With the full support of the U.S. Navy behind him, MacArthur and his Sixth Army would be able to fulfill his promise to return to the Philippines. The success of the land battles was dependent upon the victories at sea.

The Imperial Japanese Navy knew that if they lost the Philippines to the Americans, they would also lose the war. In an attempt to protect their stronghold, the IJN drew up a plan of action that risked their remaining surface ships, yet if successful, gave them a chance to destroy the American Invasion fleet and isolate the Allied ground forces on Leyte. The plan involved the use of decoy ships to draw off the main American covering force while two powerful battleship forces would penetrate the Central Philippines and converge on Leyte Gulf.

Japanese Forces

Northern Force (Main Body) – Vice Admiral Jisaburo Ozawa - "Decoy Force"

> 1 CV – *Zuikaku*
>
> 3 CVLs – *Zuiho, Chitose, Chiyoda*
>
> 2 BBs – *Ise and Hyuga*
>
> 3 CLs – *Isuzu, Tama, Oyoda*
>
> 8 DDs

Center Force – Vice Admiral Takeo Kurita (The main Japanese force in the battle, although the Northern "decoy" force was referred to as the "main body" by the Japanese.)

> 5 BBs – *Yamato, Mushashi, Nagato, Kongo, Haruna*
>
> 10 CAs – *Atago, Takao, Chokai, Maya, Myoko, Haguro, Kumano, Suzuya, Chikuma, Tone*
>
> 2 CLs – *Noshiro, Yahagi*

15 DDs

Southern Force – Vice Admirals Shoji Nishimura and Kiyohide Shima – consisted of two groups, the larger force, commanded by Nishimura and the smaller striking force, commanded by Shima.

Nishimura's Force:

2 BBs – *Fuso, Yamashiro*

1 CA – *Mogami*

4 DDs

Shima's Striking Force:

2 CAs – *Nachi, Ashigara*

1 CL – *Abukuma*

7 DDs

On October 23, 1944, submarines operating off Borneo, Palawan, and Manila spotted and reported an approaching Japanese fleet. Little did MacArthur know that in five days' time, Japan planned to employ its entire armada to destroy his Seventh Fleet Invasion Force at its anchorage at Leyte Gulf. Halsey's Task Force 38's carrier group had struck Formosa to the north, and had returned toward Leyte in support of MacArthur.

Meanwhile, Admiral Ozawa's decoy force sortied from its base in Japan, shadowing Halsey's ships. Ozawa fully intended to use his remaining planes against the task force, but his strategy was to utilize his fleet as bait to lure the American carriers away from Leyte Gulf.

American Forces – Third and Seventh Fleets

Third Fleet – Covering and Support Forces

Admiral William "Bull" Halsey – Third Fleet was assigned to cover and support Seventh Fleet, and was under overall command of Admiral Chester Nimitz. Task Force 38 of Third Fleet, was commanded by Admiral Marc Mitscher and divided into four fast carrier groups:

Task Group 38.1 – Vice Admiral John S. McCain, Commander (at Ulithi)

Task Group 38.2 – Rear Admiral Gerald F. Bogan, Commander

Task Group 38.3 – Rear Admiral Frederick C. Sherman, Commander (*Santa Fe* in this group)

Task Group 38.4 – Rear Admiral Ralph E. Davison, Commander

Seventh Fleet- Leyte Landing Forces

Seventh Fleet, commanded by Vice Admiral Thomas Kincaid, was under the overall command of General Douglas MacArthur, and consisted of just under 200 ships of all types and purposes, including a powerful force of escort carriers, cruisers and battleships and a large number of destroyers.

During the Leyte Campaign, the command was divided between Admiral Halsey and General MacArthur. Poor cooperation and communication between the two commanders led to great confusion in the ensuing battle.

The ships of the Third and Seventh Naval Fleets joined together to meet the oncoming foe and engaged in four separate battles, three occurring almost simultaneously. These battles, known collectively as the Battle of Leyte Gulf, were as follows:

- Sibuyan Sea – October 24, 1944
- Surigao Strait – October 25, 1944
- Battle off Samar – October 25, 1944
- Cape Engaño – October 25-26, 1944

Submarine Action in Palawan Passage: October 22-23, 1944

A huge convoy of Japanese warships steamed toward Leyte Gulf. Kurita's Center Force consisted of five battleships, ten heavy cruisers, two light cruisers, and 15 destroyers.

According to intelligence reports, the Japanese Second Fleet left its anchorage at Singapore, but Kurita's ships somehow disappeared at sea. Scout planes scoured the seas but failed to locate the enemy warships. At midnight, two American submarines, *Darter* and *Dace*, located the Center Force passing Palawan Island and immediately reported their findings to Admiral Kincaid's Seventh Fleet. The subs torpedoed the heavy cruiser, *Atago*, Admiral Kurita's flagship, and made two hits on the *Takao*. The next target was the heavy cruiser *Maya*, hit by four torpedoes. *Atago* and *Maya* both sank while the crippled *Takao*, with two destroyers, left the fray shadowed by the two U.S. submarines attempting to finish her off.

During the hunt, *Darter* ran aground and she was eventually abandoned, with the *Dace* taking on her entire crew. *Atago* sank so swiftly that *Kurita* was forced into the waters, and transferred to the battleship *Yamato*. The Japanese fleet proceeded on to the Sibuyan Sea.

Sibuyan Sea Battle: October 24, 1944

The *Darter* and *Dace* report was just what Halsey needed to instigate his own search. Around 8:00 a.m. on the morning of October 24, scout planes from the *Santa Fe* and her Task Group 38.3 first discovered Kurita's Center Force entering the Sibuyan Sea. Hellcat fighters, dive bombers, and torpedo planes from the *Enterprise* (Task Group 38.4) were first to strike the enemy ships. Next came planes from the carriers *Intrepid* and *Cabot* (Task Group 38.2), striking and crippling the heavy cruiser *Myoko* and scoring hits on the battleships *Nagato*, *Yamato*, and *Musashi*. Minutes later, a second wave from *Intrepid*, including the *Essex* and *Lexington* (both carriers of Task Group 38.3), zeroed in on the *Musashi*, giving her ten more hits.

While the damaged *Mushasi*, now listing to port, withdrew to her base, another wave from the *Enterprise* and *Franklin* (Task Group 38.4) hit the giant battleship with additional bombs and torpedoes. Swinging his fleet around out of aircraft range, Kurita's Center Force passed the crippled *Musashi* as his fleet retreated to regroup. After being struck by numerous bombs and torpedoes, *Musashi* finally capsized and sank that night. Almost 1,000 men went down with her.

U.S. pilots overestimated the number of ships sunk and left the area believing they had completely neutralized Kurita's fleet. The sunken battleship *Musashi* and the heavy cruiser *Myoko,* forced out of the battle, were the only capital ships significantly damaged in the attack. Halsey concluded that the Japanese fleet was no longer a threat to American forces at Leyte. However, Kurita's change of course was temporary, and his Center Force remained a powerful concentration of naval might.

While the planes from Task Groups 38.2, 38.3, and 38.4 attacked Kurita's Center Force in the Sibuyan Sea, Admiral Sherman's ships in Task Group 38.3, northeast of Luzon Island, took the brunt of an enemy air attack from the island's land-based planes—the Japanese First Air Fleet. Vice Admiral Takijiro Onishi directed three strike waves from Luzon. Each consisted of about 30-40 planes now swooping down on the *Santa Fe* and her companion ships.

Some of the invaders were broken by the CAP (U.S. Combat Air Patrol), but others continued to close in until the radar screen became so cluttered inside the eight-mile circle that *Santa Fe* and Task Group 38.3 had to depend on visual sighting. *Santa Fe's* anti-aircraft battery—five-inch, 40mm, and 20 mm—fired continually. The enemy planes vectored for target gave Ridgeway and his fellow gunners a strenuous workout. After enemy formations were broken up, lone planes broke through the low cloud cover scoring near misses, and still more raids were reported closing in.

At 9:38 a.m., one of the dive bombers slipped through the defenses, and the light carrier *Princeton* took a direct hit forcing her out of the line. A series of violent explosions engulfed the hangar deck in flames. Light cruiser *Birmingham* began directing the fire-fighting on the *Princeton* while the crew abandoned their burning ship. Suddenly, *Princeton* was racked by a huge explosion, throwing deadly shrapnel onto the crowded decks of the *Birmingham*. The explosion killed 129 men and injured 236, adding to the more than 100 hundred casualties on the *Princeton*.

Efforts to save the *Princeton* failed. Members of the remaining crew were recovered, and the light cruiser *Reno* finally scuttled the ship with torpedoes early in the evening of October 24. USS *Princeton* was the largest American ship lost during the Battle of Leyte Gulf.

While it was clear the Americans had been fighting land-based attackers approaching from the northwest (Luzon), planes from an undetected Japanese carrier force were now descending on the group. The *Essex* and *Lexington* launched search planes as the furious attack continued. Apparently, the attackers came from Ozawa's carriers, yet to be discovered.

At noon, in the midst of launching and recovery operations, a new series of land-based attacks began. Again, the sky swarmed with planes. Extra fighters launched and broke up two raids, but one group got through and into the formation. Simultaneously, three dive-bombers roared in seemingly from nowhere, and a torpedo bomber made a run. *Santa Fe* port and starboard batteries immediately opened fire. The formation emergency-turned, zigzagged, and evaded; luckily, no hits scored.

Late afternoon, the search planes from *Essex* and *Lexington* (Task Group 38.3) reported a large Japanese carrier force 190 miles to the northeast and notified Admiral Halsey. When Ozawa's bait ships were discovered, Halsey made the momentous decision to leave San Bernardino Strait in order to crush this fresh enemy fleet.

Convinced that Kurita's Center Force was in full retreat, and that the Japanese would not launch a major operation without carrier support, Halsey was certain the Northern Force was now the main threat. However, he was unaware that Ozawa's carrier fleet was a spent force with only 30 or so planes to spare. In the Sibuyan Sea, Halsey's Third Fleet flew over 250 sorties against Kurita's fleet. Still, the mighty warships of Center Force were a powerhouse that would later threaten Admiral Kincaid's "baby" carriers of Taffy 3 off San Bernardino Strait.

San Bernardino Strait Left Unguarded: Communication Breakdown

Tired of "babysitting" for MacArthur's Invasion Force at Leyte, "Bull" was ready to charge Ozawa's oncoming fleet. Recently, Halsey's standing orders to guard the San Bernardino Strait had been modified by Admiral Nimitz, giving him the freedom to initiate an attack against the enemy fleet if the opportunity presented itself. Halsey's greatest ambition was to strike the Japanese and annihilate their carriers. Here lay the opportunity to push Nimitz's mandate to its limit. Unfortunately, Halsey's following decisions would ignite a series of confused communications and misunderstandings among the Allied Commanders regarding the strategic movements of Ozawa and the location of Kurita's force, as well as the guarding of San Bernardino Strait.

Within an hour after contact was made with Ozawa's ships, Halsey planned for the attack and quickly developed a strategy to cover San Bernardino Strait. A powerful force of fast surface ships, designated Task Force 34, consisting of four battleships, five cruisers, and 14 destroyers, under the command of Vice Admiral Willis A. "Ching" Lee, would be the covering group.

Late afternoon, October 24, Halsey telegraphed an ambiguously worded message to his task group commanders regarding what he later officially reported as his "contingency" battle plan for the establishment of Task Force 34. However, he failed to give details as to "when-and-under-what-circumstances" this task force would be activated. The task group commanders, and both Admiral Nimitz at Pacific Fleet Headquarters and Admiral King at Washington, D.C., were now under the impression that Task Force 34 was formed and in position.

Five hours later, Halsey sent a follow-up message, attempting to clarify his intentions that this was a battle plan regarding the formation of TF 34 in case of surface action. Unfortunately, Halsey's second message was sent by voice radio and was not intercepted by Admiral Kincaid of the Seventh Fleet. Halsey also failed to notify Nimitz or King. The result would cause a domino effect on the course of subsequent battles that occurred at Leyte Gulf.

Believing that in the Sibuyan Sea the Japanese battleships had been knocked out of the fight and that Ozawa's carrier force was the main threat, on the afternoon of October 24, Halsey ordered a full-scale pursuit for the following morning. He radioed Nimitz and Kincaid:

"CENTRAL FORCE HEAVILY DAMAGED ACCORDING TO STRIKE REPORTS. AM PROCEEDING NORTH WITH THREE GROUPS TO ATTACK CARRIER FORCES AT DAWN."

His message was once again misleading, especially when paired with the previous miscommunication. Kincaid and Nimitz were now under the assumption that Task Force 34, under Admiral Lee, had been formed as a separate entity to guard San Bernardino Strait. However, Task Force 34 had not been formed and detached. Instead, Lee's battleships proceeded north with Halsey's Third Fleet carriers in pursuit of Ozawa. San Bernardino Strait had been left with no U.S. ships to guard the passage.

Early on the morning of October 25, Halsey detached three of his four carrier groups, the northernmost Task Groups 38.2, 38.3 and 38.4, for airstrikes against Ozawa's Northern Fleet. Six battleships and seven cruisers, including the *Santa Fe,* sailed ahead of the carriers to be ready for gun action. At daybreak, the carriers began launching strikes. The decoy plan was a success. Not only had Halsey been lured into a "snipe" hunt, but Kurita's threatening Center Force was steaming through San Bernardino Strait on its way to attack MacArthur's amphibious and landing forces at Leyte.

Throughout the night, Halsey ignored messages received from carrier *Independence's* night reconnaissance aircraft—and again relayed to him by Admiral Bogan of Task Group 38.2—that Ozawa's ships were a decoy force. Admiral Lee came to the same conclusion and indicated this by blinker message to Halsey's flagship, but he, too, was brushed off. The next morning, American scout planes made contact with Kurita's Center Force and immediately notified Halsey, who had left San Bernardino Strait wide open for the Japanese ships. The American carriers and battleships rushed back south to intercept Kurita's Center Force, which had already made it through the Strait.

While the cruisers and destroyers of Task Group 38.3 steamed toward Ozawa's Northern Force, Admiral Kincaid's Seventh Fleet had more than his northern flank to be concerned about—Nishimura's force was about to attack Kincaid's southern flank through the Surigao Strait.

Surigao Strait: October 25, 1944

Headed for Surigao Strait during darkness was Nishimura's Southern Force with its two battleships, *Yamashiro* and *Fuso*, followed fifty miles to the rear by Shima's Fifth Fleet, which included the two heavy cruisers *Nachi* and *Ashigara*. Although the Americans lost track of Kurita's Center Force, their aircraft had spotted Nishimura's warships, confirming suspicion that an attack was about to be made on Leyte Gulf through the Surigao Strait. The day prior (October 24), after Southern Force had been detected, every ship in the Seventh Fleet was alerted by Admiral Kincaid to expect a night attack.

In Leyte Gulf, U.S. transports and amphibious ships unloaded their men and supplies. Included in this group was the cruiser on which General MacArthur was headquartered. A screen of escort destroyers and patrol boats was ordered to surround the American ships, and all traffic in and out of the Gulf was terminated at sunset.

Since the Japanese would enter the Surigao Strait at night, Admiral Jesse Oldendorf knew the defense of Leyte would fall upon his battleships, cruisers, destroyers and PT boats. Oldendorf planned to strike first with his PT boats and destroyers and finish them off from the fire of the cruisers and battleships. He deployed his light forces on each flank of the approaching column and sealed off the enemy's advance through the strait with his fleet "heavies."

The main battle line was six battleships steaming east and west across Surigao Strait. North of the battleships toward Leyte Gulf lay a screen of six destroyers to guard against enemy subs. To the south toward the strait was a force of cruisers, with destroyers, and Patrol Torpedo (PT) boats on the right and left flank used as pickets to find the enemy. This classic naval maneuver of "crossing the T" was the fulfillment of every fleet commander's dream. The formation would enable the U.S. battleships and cruisers to concentrate fire broadsides while restricting the enemy ships the use of only their forward guns until they maneuvered into position. By then, it would be too late. In the ensuing battle, the Japanese would lose a battleship and three destroyers almost before they opened fire.

While passing the cape of Panaon Island, Nishimura and Shima's Southern Force ran into the deadly trap set for them by Oldendorf's Seventh Fleet, consisting of the battleships *Mississippi, West Virginia, Maryland, Tennessee, California,* and *Pennsylvania,* eight cruisers (heavy cruisers *Louisville, Portland, Minneapolis,* and

HMAS *Shropshire*, light cruisers *Denver, Columbia, Phoenix,* and *Boise*), 28 destroyers and 39 Patrol Torpedo boats. To pass Surigao Strait and reach the landings, Nishimura's force would have to dodge torpedoes from the PT boats, evade two groups of destroyers, proceed up the strait under the concentrated fire of six battleships in line across the far mouth of the strait, and finally break through the screen of cruisers.

The PT boats made first contact with the Japanese ships. Nishimura's battle fleet passed through the PT gauntlet unscathed for the next few hours, dodging one torpedo after another. One American patrol boat was lost, but the others continued their reports to Oldendorf's waiting warships. As the Japanese Southern Force entered Surigao Strait, the destroyers were next to attack on both flanks, launching a full-scale torpedo attack.

Battleship *Fuso* was hit, fell out of formation, and sank. A few minutes later, a second group of American destroyers launched their torpedoes striking three Japanese destroyers, one sunk and the remaining two were knocked out of the fight. The battleship *Yamashiro,* also struck, continued to steam on. Of the original Japanese column, only *Yamashiro*, cruiser *Mogami*, and a destroyer remained in line. Southern Force now faced the American cruisers and battleships with only one-fourth of their original number.

As Nishimura's ships approached the "crossing of the T," American cruisers and battleships lay in wait. The cruisers opened fire first, followed by the battleships. Among the six battleships, *Tennessee, West Virginia,* and *California* executed most of the shooting. All three ships had been damaged during the Pearl Harbor attack and received total reconstructions with the latest radar. The *Mogami* and *Yamashiro* took hit after hit. Within five minutes after the Americans opened fire, both ships left the battle. Finally, the battleship *Yamashiro* sank, taking Admiral Nishimura with her and almost all hands. Only the burning cruiser *Mogami* and one destroyer retreated back down the Surigao Strait.

At this point, Admiral Shima's Fifth Fleet, which had been trailing Nishimura's force, began to enter the strait. After one of his ships was torpedoed by a PT boat, Shima quickly retreated from the area. Oldendorf's ships pursued the fleeing Japanese and fired their last shots around 7 a.m., sinking the destroyer *Asagumo,* which had been torpedoed and damaged earlier.

Soon after U.S. forces retreated the battle, an astonished Oldendorf received news that Seventh Fleet's escorts carriers had come under a surprise attack off Samar by Kurita's Center Force. The U.S. Invasion ships and the entire Leyte Gulf operation now lay in harm's way.

CHAPTER EIGHTEEN

BATTLES OFF SAMAR AND CAPE ENGANO

Battle off Samar- "David vs. Goliath": October 25, 1944

Ozawa's decoy fleet had successfully drawn Halsey's entire Third Fleet away from the Philippines, and early morning of October 25, Kurita's Center Force had slipped through San Bernardino Strait with no opposition to their front. Admiral Kurita's battleship force steamed toward Leyte Gulf. In spite of losses at Palawan Passage and Sibuyan Sea, Kurita's fleet was still a threat.

The defense of Leyte was now left to the anti-submarine warships of Rear Admiral Thomas Sprague, Overall Commander of

Task Unit 77.4, consisting of three escort carrier task units, known as the "three Taffies," because of their radio call signs:

Taffy 1 Group – Rear Admiral Thomas Sprague, Commander

Taffy 2 Group – Rear Admiral Felix P. Stump, Commander

Taffy 3 Group – Rear Admiral Clifton A. F. "Ziggy" Sprague, Commander

Taffy's "tin cans" had been designed as support and supply ships, not enemy combat vessels. Their primary mission in the Philippines Reoccupation Plan was to screen for submarines in the area and launch ground attack aircraft to support MacArthur's Invasion Force.

Ridgeway's nephew, Lew Painter, had joined the Navy in 1942, and was a fireman on the *Fanshaw Bay,* the flagship of Taffy 3. Lew would be in the heat of the battle as Admiral Kurita's powerful warships directed toward Leyte Gulf. As the sun rose on October 25, Taffy 3, east of Samar, steamed north as the Northern Air Support Group. Taffy 2, in the central position, patrolled off the entrance to Leyte Gulf, while Taffy 1 covered the southern approaches.

During dawn patrol, Taffy 3's lookouts observed anti-aircraft fire to the north, and minutes later came under intense fire from Kurita's powerful Center Force consisting of four battleships (*Yamato, Kongo, Nagato,* and *Haruna*), six heavy and two light cruisers, and 11 destroyers. To survive, Taffy 3's little group of ships would have to slow the advance of the fast-approaching enemy and then withdraw toward Leyte Gulf for much needed help.

Admiral Clifton "Ziggy" Sprague, Commander of Taffy 3, knew his "baby carriers" were the sole defense between the advancing

Japanese armada and MacArthur's invasion force at Leyte. The brave crew of Taffy 3 mustered all their courage and determined to fight the oncoming Goliath. Sprague's carriers turned into the wind, launched their aircraft, then hightailed it toward Leyte through a storm of enemy shells, hoping against hope they would soon be assisted by the big boys. Minutes later, enormous shells from the 18-inch guns of the giant battleship *Yamato* threw up a huge column of water close to Sprague's flagship, *Fanshaw Bay*.

Meanwhile, the destroyers *Johnston, Hoel* and *Heerman* had bravely turned to attack Kurita's battleships and heavy cruisers. Immediately, Captain Ernest E. Evans of the *Johnston* took the lead and made smoke to conceal the escort carriers of Taffy 3. *Johnston's* gunnery officer, Lt. Robert C. Hagen, later reported, "...we felt like 'little David' without a sling shot."

Captain Evans, with his guns and torpedoes out of range, closed in and opened with his five-inch battery at the closest enemy cruiser, firing over 200 rounds in five minutes. Ten torpedoes were launched toward the oncoming ships, then he reversed course to hide behind the smoke screen as the enemy zeroed in on the *Johnston*. Power to the three aft five-inch guns, to the steering, and to the *Johnston's* compass were all knocked out by multiple hits. Evans headed for the covering of an oncoming rain storm and made rapid repairs.

Just before 8 a.m., Admiral Clifton Sprague ordered Taffy 3's destroyers to launch a torpedo attack.

With her torpedoes spent, the *Johnston* could only provide fire support with her remaining five-inch cannons and other anti-aircraft guns. Evans, a Cherokee Native American, had vowed never to take one step back from the Japanese, no matter the cost, and so joined in the attack. When Taffy 3 exited the smoke screen, they were face to face with the pagoda superstructure of the *Kongo*. *Kongo* opened her big guns at the tin cans, remarkably scoring no hits. Minutes later, the *Johnston* miraculously scored multiple hits on the *Kongo*.

Meanwhile, Captain Evans noticed that *Gambier Bay* (CVE-73) in the American carrier group had been singled out by an enemy cruiser, and ordered his crippled ship to draw fire turning the attention away from *Gambier Bay*. The *Johnston* scored four hits on the cruiser, but then Evans spotted a Japanese destroyer division descending on the entire carrier group of Taffy 3. Evans turned toward the lead ship, firing on her, stopping her cold, then turned to the second ship in line, breaking up the Japanese column and distracting their aim. Every enemy torpedo missed its mark. However, during Evan's brave charge to protect the American carriers, the *Johnston* took several hits, knocking out guns, burning her bridge, and exploding magazines.

Losing all power, USS *Johnston* was now dead in the water encircled by Japanese ships, firing at will. Eventually, she rolled over and began to sink. A single enemy destroyer pumped a final shot into the expiring ship to finish her off. The Japanese captain was observed saluting the USS *Johnston* as she sank. The valiant Captain Evans, alive in the water when his ship sank, was never heard from again.

With the loss of the *Johnston*, Taffy 3 was left with only two destroyers, *Hoel* and *Heerman*, and four destroyer escorts, *Samuel B. Roberts*, *Raymond*, *Dennis*, and *Butler*, to carry on the attack. *Hoel*, closing in on the *Kongo*, opened fire with her cannons, and launched half her torpedoes—all misses. Return fire from *Kongo* struck the *Hoel*, knocking out her port engine, radar, and steering controls. Undaunted, *Hoel* manually fired her last torpedoes at the approaching cruiser *Haguro*, inflicting some damage. *Hoel* now found herself in the same situation as the *Johnston* had earlier encountered. Surrounded by the enemy, the destroyer continued firing her guns in attempt to draw fire on herself and away from the carriers. Listing to port and slowing sinking by the stern, orders were given to abandon ship as the *Hoel* rolled over and sank.

In a final, desperate attempt, *Heerman*, the last of Taffy 3's destroyers, charged into the teeth of gunfire from the Japanese battleships and cruisers as the "baby carriers" launched their last planes and formed a defensive circle sailing south. Beginning a run through enemy shells, *Heerman* directed her five-inch guns at the heavy cruiser *Chikuma*, launched a spread of torpedoes at the heavy cruiser *Haguro*, then changed course north to engage the four battleships. Her first target was the lead ship, *Kongo*. *Heerman* sent three torpedoes her way. The *Haruna* was the target of her last torpedoes. Believing that one "fish" had hit the battleship, *Heerman* dodged salvos as she raced toward her carriers to lay another protective smoke screen.

The Japanese ships were forced repeatedly to take evasive action which slowed down their advance. During the melee, the giant battleship *Yamato*, caught between two torpedo spreads, reversed course. Admiral Kurita led the flagship out of the battle line to avoid taking hits. Kurita, thinking he was fighting the "big boys", ordered a general attack and lost contact with the battle.

A few minutes later, *Heerman* charged back into the fight, placing herself between the tiny escort carriers and the column of four enemy heavy cruisers. She faced off again with the *Chikuma*, with both ships seriously damaged. A series of hits knocked out one of *Heerman's* guns and flooded the ship's forward part. The combined effect of *Heerman's* firepower, plus the bombs and strafing from carrier-based planes, forced *Chikuma* to withdraw. *Chikuma* would later sink during her flight. As she retreated, *Heerman* was now trading shells with the heavy cruiser *Tone* until the destroyer reached a position suitable to resume laying smoke for her carriers.

The CVEs returned enemy fire with all the firepower they had—one five-inch gun per carrier. The *Fanshaw Bay* fired on a cruiser and was believed to have registered five hits. The *Kalinin Bay* targeted a *Nachi*-class heavy cruiser, claiming a couple of hits. The *Gambier Bay* claimed three hits on another cruiser, and *White Plains* reported hits on multiple targets inflicting some damage.

Meanwhile, Admiral Thomas Sprague, Overall Commander, ordered all escort carriers from his three Taffy units to immediately launch any remaining aircraft. Then the fighters from Admiral Stump's Taffy 2 zoomed in striking the *Tone*, and she, too, broke off action and fled. As the carriers of Taffy 3 turned south retreating through gunfire, USS *Gambier Bay*, at the rear of the formation, became the target of the giant battleship *Yamato* and took multiple hits. She capsized a little after 9:00 a.m. Several other Taffy 3 carriers, though damaged, managed to escape.

The courageous destroyers and carrier planes saved the day for the "little Davids" of the Taffy 3. Against all odds, they held off Kurita's giant warships with only six escort carriers, three destroyers, and four destroyer escorts. Taffy 3's losses were 792 men dead and 768 wounded. As the desperate action was coming to a close, Admiral Takijiro Onishi launched kamikaze attacks from Luzon against the Allied ships in Leyte Gulf and the Taffy escort carrier units off Samar. *St. Lo* of Taffy 3 was hit by a kamikaze plane and sank.

Samuel Morison, the U.S. Naval historian, would later write,

> *"In no engagement in its entire history has the United States Navy shown more gallantry, guts and gumption than in those two morning hours between 0730 and 0930 off Samar..."*

Admiral Kurita, under the assumption that his ships had been engaging with major fleet units rather than small escort carriers and destroyers, broke off the fight and missed his opportunity to attack the shipping at Leyte Gulf. Instead, he went in hot pursuit of American carriers purportedly sailing to the north of his fleet. However, without air scouts, Kurita was unable to make contact with the ships.

Kincaid's Cries for Help

Throughout the morning of October 25, desperate calls for assistance had been sent to Halsey from Kincaid's Seventh Fleet, who had been engaging Nishimura's Southern Force in the Surigao Strait since 2:00 a.m. and Kurita's Center Force all morning. Halsey, misjudging the gravity of the situation, had delayed sending the desperately needed assistance.

Meanwhile, Admiral Nimitz, 3,000 miles away at Pearl Harbor, had been monitoring Taffy 3's cries for help, and sent an encrypted message to Halsey asking the whereabouts of Task Force 34. When Halsey finally realized Ozawa's fleet was a diversion, he ordered Lee's Task Force 34, who were almost within gun range of Ozawa's ships, to revert course to San Bernardino Strait to assist Seventh Fleet. By the time TF 34 arrived, the Taffy battle was over and they missed the chance to intercept the Japanese Center Force. Kurita's surviving fleet had escaped through the strait. Of his original five battleships, only the *Yamato* remained battle-worthy.

Meanwhile, far to the north, the U.S. Third Fleet was attacking Ozawa's decoy force in the Battle off Cape Engaño (so named from the nearest point of land at the northeastern tip of Luzon Island).

Battle off Cape Engaño – October 25-26, 1944

Ozawa Attacked

Halsey's Task Force 38 steamed toward Cape Engano to eliminate Ozawa's fleet, which consisted of four carriers (*Zuikaku, Zuiho, Chitose*, and *Chiyoda*), two battleships (*Hyuga* and *Ise*), three light cruisers (*Oyodo, Tama*, and *Isuzu*), nine destroyers, with few carrier planes. Task Force 38 had five large fleet carriers (*Intrepid, Franklin, Lexington, Enterprise*, and *Essex*), five light carriers

(*Independence, Belleau Wood, Langley, Cabot,* and *San Jacinto*), six battleships (*Alabama, Iowa, Massachusetts, New Jersey, South Dakota,* and *Washington*), eight cruisers (two heavy and six light, including *Santa Fe*), and more than 40 destroyers. The ten U.S. carriers had almost 1,000 planes.

Halsey passed tactical command of Task Force 38 to Admiral Mitscher, who ordered the American carrier groups to launch their first strike wave of 180 aircraft at dawn on October 26, before the Northern Force had been located. Search planes sighted Ozawa's ships off Cape Engaño around 7:00 a.m., and by now the first strike wave was on the attack. At 8:00 a.m., the bombers and torpedo planes roared in and continued strikes until evening. Meanwhile, their escorting fighters destroyed Ozawa's remaining combat air patrol of about 30 planes.

In the day's work, Task Force 38 had flown just over 500 sorties against the Northern Force, sinking the carrier *Zuikaku* (Ozawa's flagship), and damaging the light carriers *Chitose* and *Zuiho*, and one destroyer. They also crippled light carrier *Chiyoda* and cruiser *Tama*. Ozawa transferred his flag to the light cruiser *Oyodo*.

Santa Fe's Actions Off Cape Engaño: October 25, 1944

As soon as Task Force 34 and her carrier group returned to Surigao Strait, Admiral Dubose's Cruiser Division 13 (*Santa Fe, Mobile, Wichita,* and *New Orleans*), along with 12 destroyers was detached to catch and destroy the Japanese ships. *Santa Fe* led the charge. Shortly after 2:00 p.m., the light striking group set a course for the nearest Japanese ship sighted by carrier planes. Around 4:00

p.m., a surface target was picked up on the radar screen. As contact closed, the light carrier, *Chitose,* was observed on the horizon slightly down by the bow, but not burning.

All four American cruisers commenced firing when range allowed, and almost immediately the *Chitose* took hits and started to burn. No planes could be seen on the carrier, but men were swarming all over the flight deck, sliding down hand lines into the sea, and scrambling off the radio antenna. Steadily and methodically, the cruisers' projectiles mauled the carrier. *Chitose* slowly capsized and finally went under. With *Chitose* burning and sinking, the cruisers were free to continue the chase.

Now that the sun was down, the men topside could see nothing, but the radar scope showed three pips milling around, with the distance rapidly closing. The light cruisers, *Santa Fe* and *Mobile,* directed fire at the nearest target, while the heavy cruisers the more distant targets. The five-inch mounts began illuminating with star shells as the *Santa Fe* closed to almost point-blank range and resumed fire. Four minutes later the target was dead in the water. The range was 400 yards now, and the majority of each salvo could not fail to hit—a single ship was sunk. Although accurate identification was impossible, observers agreed the target was a cruiser of the *Oyodo* or *Agano* class.

At 8:10 p.m., the night fighters reported the nearest target was 42 miles north. Since the fuel situation in the destroyers precluded a 30-knot stern chase, CruDiv 13 ordered the force to rejoin the carrier groups. After refueling the next day, the *Santa Fe* resumed her previous station with Task Group 38.3. The light cruiser lay off Leyte Gulf in a covering position until October 28 when she was ordered to proceed to Ulithi.

The *"Lucky Lady"* now had her 11th Battle Star, and Ridgeway had received lucky star number 13.

Leyte Gulf Conclusion

Meanwhile, around 11:10 p.m., an American submarine torpedoed and sank the light cruiser *Tama* of Ozawa's force. This was the last action in the Battle off Cape Engaño, and after some final airstrikes on the retreating Japanese forces on October 26, the Battle for Leyte Gulf ended.

A majority of the remaining Japanese surface fleet had been destroyed, ending the Empire's ability to move resources from Southeast Asia to her home islands. Japanese losses included four aircraft carriers, three battleships, six heavy and four light cruisers, and eleven destroyers, along with several hundred aircraft and over 10,500 sailors. Allied losses included one light carrier, two escort carriers, two destroyers and one destroyer escort.

CHAPTER NINETEEN

LEYTE AFTERMATH ACTIONS

Luzon and East Leyte Strikes – November 1 – Dec. 14, 1944

Santa Fe reached Ulithi Lagoon, on October 30, 1944, and Captain Harold C. Fitz replaced Captain Wright as her commanding officer.

On November 1, the *Santa Fe* departed Ulithi Port, with Task Group 38.3, headed for Manus of the Admiralties that evening, when she received orders to proceed west to engage heavy enemy surface forces reportedly approaching Leyte Gulf. On November 3, while traveling through heavily mined waters, a Japanese sub attacked the group. The USS *Reno* took a torpedo hit and retired to port. The report of enemy surface ships approaching Leyte proved false. Consequently, airstrikes were ordered against Luzon in the Philippines instead.

Land-based Japanese air power, though well-reduced, still possessed the capability for determined attacks against the U.S. forces at Leyte. On November 5, Task Group 38.3's air fighters hit Manila. At the same time, the Japanese kamikaze planes attacked the formation just after twelve noon. One crashed on the *Lexington*, another near the *Ticonderoga*, while a third was shot down.

Manila was hit again on November 6, after which *Santa Fe* and her task force retired eastward to fuel. On November 10, the carriers headed west to counter Japanese forces reportedly in the area, but the attack failed to materialize. Afterward, the carrier planes struck enemy shipping in the Visayan area.

Search planes launched on November 11, located a Japanese convoy in the Camotes Sea (Central Visayas). One strike each from the three U.S. carrier task groups annihilated the enemy ships. Sustained strikes were executed on the Manila area November 14, then the *Santa Fe* headed to Ulithi with the carriers, arriving November 17, 1944.

While anchored at Ulithi on November 20, midget submarines crept into Ulithi Lagoon, and one torpedoed the U.S. tanker *Mississinewa*. A *Santa Fe* Kingfisher, flying patrol at the time, landed near the blazing vessel and hauled several survivors clear before rescue boats arrived on the scene.

On November 22, the *Santa Fe* sortied from Ulithi as part of Task Group 38.3 for airstrikes on the Philippines. As the U.S. planes hit enemy shipping on Luzon's west coast November 25, Japanese planes targeted the *Santa Fe's* force. One suicide attacker dove

220

through the anti-aircraft screen and crashed onto the carrier *Essex*. *Santa Fe* splashed a second suicider. The Japanese heavily attacked the adjacent task groups, resulting in two U.S. ships taking kamikaze crash-dives. East of the Philippines, Task Group 38.3 operated in a supporting position until December 2, 1944, after which the group returned to Ulithi.

Santa Fe, with Task Group 38.3 left Ulithi December 10, commissioned to prevent Japanese use of their airfields while the Mindoro landings progressed. On December 14th, the carriers launched strikes over the entire Luzon area. An umbrella of "fly-boys" from the carriers covered the Luzon airfields day and night, successfully repelling the Japanese air forces while MacArthur's troops landed on Mindoro. Enemy planes and ships suffered a high toll.

Halsey's Typhoon

Around the 17th of December, 1944, a vicious storm suddenly developed about 300 miles off the Philippines and caught Task Force 38 of Halsey's Third Fleet off guard. The ships had completed their air support for the Mindoro invasion, and Halsey planned to refuel his ships the next two days in preparation for a three-day airstrike on Manila to begin on December 19. Fueling at sea to the east was violently interrupted when the bottom dropped out of the barometer with rising swells and 100 mile-per-hour winds.

Weather reports given to Halsey throughout the 17th proved inaccurate as he radically changed courses to avoid the killer storm. On December 18, his fleet ran straight into the brunt of the typhoon's

150 mile-per-hour winds. Halsey's heavy fleet weathered the storm, but the rest of his ships were scattered across the Philippine Sea. Three destroyers (*Spence, Hull* and *Monaghan*) capsized and sank. Several carriers suffered fires in their hangars, and almost 150 planes wrecked or were blown overboard. The carrier *Monterey* was nearly destroyed by her own planes as they crashed into bulkheads, exploding violently. Dozens of Third Fleet's ships were badly damaged and sent back to Ulithi for repairs.

Surviving the pounding wind and churning water that at one point sent her rolling 50 degrees to starboard, the *Santa Fe* once again became the "*Lucky Lady.*"

On December 18, when the storm's nucleus passed, the *Santa Fe* and other ships of Task Force 38 remained in the operational area searching for survivors of the three sunken destroyers. Almost 800 lives were lost in a battle where the sea always wins. The American Navy had not suffered such harm since the Battle of Savo Island, when more than 1200 U.S. sailors and officers lost their lives.

Weather continued to be unfavorable causing another air approach on Luzon to abort. One last sweep was made for men of the lost destroyers before Third Fleet limped back into Ulithi on Christmas Eve, December 24, 1944.

Third Fleet Supporting Operations: January 3 – 22, 1945

Formosa and Luzon Strikes: January 3 – 6, 1945

On December 30, the *Santa Fe,* with the fast carriers of Task Force 38, proceeded northwest from Ulithi with orders to attack Japanese forces in the Lingayen area. Despite continually bad weather, surprise airstrikes were launched at Formosa January 3, 4, and 5, 1945. Luzon was hit on the 6th. Another strike on Formosa was scheduled for January 7. Three days of carrier strikes, consisting of over 1300 sorties, left Formosa burning.

Strikes leading up to Iwo Jima: Remainder of January 1945

Indo-China and Cam Ranh Bay Strikes: January 10 & 12, 1945

While the troops were going ashore in Lingayen Gulf on January 9, 1945 (MacArthur's Luzon D-Day), Halsey's Third Fleet fast carrier task force, commanded by Admiral John McCain, struck Formosa. This target was chosen to lessen enemy air strength which had been operating against Seventh Fleet forces on earlier days. The planes of Task Force 38 hammered Formosa's airfields preventing interference with the Lingayen landings 180 miles south. That same night, Halsey ordered his fleet through the Bashi Channel (south of Formosa) into the South China Sea, leaving MacArthur's invasion forces behind on Luzon. Three passing enemy planes were shot down on January 10. E. J. Ridgeway was now 23 years young.

In continued support of the Lingayen operations, the Third Fleet fast carrier strike force made a thrust into the South China Sea to search and destroy any major units of the Japanese fleet that might be encountered there.

On January 12, the U.S. carriers launched surprise strikes on Cam Ranh Bay and Saigon, Indochina. Most enemy fleet units were absent. In one day's operations, the planes netted over 200,000 tons of vital Japanese shipping. Moving to the northwest, the force encountered heavy winds and seas, after which a two-day refueling period was required. On January 17, on the way to the fueling rendezvous, *Santa Fe* passed her 200,000-mile mark—having steamed 100,000 miles during the last eleven months.

Amroy, Takao, Swatow, Hong Kong, and Hainan (China) Strikes

Before leaving the monsoon-swept China Sea on the evening of January 20, the fast carrier task force blasted Takao on Formosa, Amoy and Swatow on the China Coast, and Hong Kong and Hainan Islands. Heavy damage was inflicted on aircraft, shipping, docks and the industrial area at Takao.

Tokyo Rose had boasted that an American fleet could never enter the China Sea. Later she changed the statement to say that a fleet once in could never get out. *Santa Fe*, with Task Force 38, had done both.

During this thrust into waters the Japanese considered their own, 3800 miles were traversed in the South China Sea with no battle damage to U.S. ships. Enemy aircraft had been unable to approach the fast carrier task force closer than 20 miles.

The *"Lucky Lady"* racked up Battle Star number 12, and Ridgeway now had 14 Battle Stars.

Around sunset on January 20, fighter planes from the American carriers successfully attacked Japanese aircraft approaching Balintang Channel in the Luzon Strait. Later, enemy planes made several light attacks on the task force but inflicted no damage.

Formosa Strike

On January 21, from a position southeast of the island, the U.S. carriers launched heavy airstrikes again at Formosa. Late that morning, without warning or previous contact, two enemy planes dove in on the formation. The *Santa Fe* fired on one of the planes that struck the *Langley*, while another plane crashed onto the *Ticonderoga*. Normal flight operations by the other carriers were resumed shortly thereafter. Other enemy air raids approached later, but none struck Task Group 38.3.

On January 22, 1945, Okinawa was hit. The destruction of enemy aircraft and airfield facilities in all these strikes led to considerable lessening of Japanese air effort against the Luzon assault forces. Afterward, Third Fleet set course toward Ulithi.

Iwo Jima Operation – February 16 – 27, 1945

The amphibious operations of the spring, summer and autumn of 1944 carried the U.S. forces such great distances across the Pacific that in February 1945 they were able to begin the assault upon the inner defenses of the Japanese Empire.

The occupation of Saipan, Tinian and Guam had established land-based air forces of the Pacific Ocean Areas in positions from which continuing air attacks could be made against Iwo Jima and Chichi Jima, and from which long-range bombers could launch against Tokyo and mainland Japan. The bombers would require fighter support in order to operate with the greatest effectiveness and a minimum of losses. Iwo Jima, 750 miles from Tokyo, provided three sites for airfields, and were ideal for the establishment of a fighter base for supporting Marianas-based B-29s. The possession of Iwo Jima would also permit medium bombers to attack Japan, deprive her of an important aerial lookout station, and reduce air attacks on the U.S. bases at the Marianas.

Admiral Halsey's command (Third Fleet) rotated to Admiral Spruance (Fifth Fleet). The Iwo Jima Invasion was supported by the fast carrier task force, commanded by Admiral Mitscher. It was anticipated that Japanese resistance would be severe. Iwo Jima had been heavily fortified by the Japanese over a period of many years as it was the only island in this strategically important group suitable for the construction of airfields.

The enemy covered the island of Iwo Jima, only five miles long and less than two miles wide, with artillery and machine gun fire, and could concentrate on the only two landing beaches. With no opportunity to select an undefended landing place, the element of surprise would be lost once the assault began. Consequently, U.S.

Naval planners prepared for what would be the most intensive ground fighting yet encountered in the Pacific. Landing forces of 60,000 Marines, put ashore by a naval force of more than 800 ships, manned by approximately 220,000 naval personnel was evidence of the scale of the attack and the expected opposition at Iwo Jima.

Tokyo Strike – February 16 – 18, 1945

By February 10, 1945, USS *Santa Fe,* with Task Group 58.4 of the fast carrier task force, was Tokyo-bound for the first carrier bombing of the Japanese capital since the Doolittle Raid in 1942. E. J. Ridgeway participated in both. From a position about 150 miles southwest of Tokyo, the carriers launched continual strikes from February 16 til noon February 17, when unfavorable weather cancelled the operation. All efforts by the enemy to damage the fleet were unsuccessful. The Japanese were finally coming to the realization that it was futile to resist. That evening Task Group 58.4 proceeded south, with the destroyers ahead, sinking several enemy pickets as they passed through their line.

This was *Santa Fe's* twelfth and last bombardment of enemy held islands. On the evening of February 18, 1945, *Santa Fe* detached for fire support at Iwo Jima.

Iwo Jima Raids and Invasion: February 19-21, 1945

Following the American occupation of the Marianas during the summer of 1944, the Japanese made every effort to turn Iwo Jima into an impregnable bastion for defense of the Japanese homeland. Naval defenses, primarily coastal defense and anti-aircraft guns, were reinforced on the island which was about 8 miles square, in the shape of a rough triangle. The extinct volcanic cone of Mount Suribachi, some 550 feet high at the apex of the triangle, towered over the landing beaches.

The target assigned for that afternoon was "Hot Rocks" or Mount Suribachi, located on the southern portion of Iwo Jima. The vicinity of Suribachi had been organized into an independent defense sector built around coastal artillery, antitank weapons, and machine guns, supported by artillery, mortars, and rocket launchers positioned at the base of the volcano. Mount Suribachi itself was full of sniper holes and mortar emplacements buried in the underground tunnels. Gunners struggled to target enemy gun positions now hidden from their view.

The *"Lucky Lady"* arrived at Iwo Jima early February 19, the day of the landing, and hundreds of American ships of all types could be seen in the early morning haze. At 6:40 a.m., the *Santa Fe* and her fleet enfiladed the southern beaches of Iwo Jima. The shelling increased as countless numbers of Marine landing craft edged toward the island. The *Santa Fe* continued firing with both five- and six-inch batteries until 10:00 a.m., and stood only 2,000 yards off shore for call fire.

For two nights, *Santa Fe* delivered harassing fire to the Japanese and kept star shells over Iwo Jima illuminating ahead of the front lines to prevent surprise counterattacks. Heavy bombardments began at dawn as American troops consolidated their positions.

Magazines were now running low, and *Santa Fe's* weary crew, having lived at their battle stations for 72 hours straight, collapsed from exhaustion. Around noon, February 21, 1945, *"Lucky Lady"* was relieved by USS *North Carolina.* Santa Fe's blistered guns had pumped over 4,000 shells into the pill boxes at Iwo Jima. The satisfied crew rejoined their carrier group.

Santa Fe had earned Battle Star number 13. E. J. Ridgeway was awarded a Bronze Star and Battle Star number 15.

CHAPTER TWENTY

TOKYO RAID, OKINAWA OPERATION & RESCUE OF USS *FRANKLIN*

Tokyo Raid: February 25-27, 1945

After replenishment, *Santa Fe,* with Mitscher's fast carrier task force, was once again headed for Tokyo on February 25, 1945, and struck the island of Hachijo, off the coast of Honshu, the following day.

The raid was carried out in bad weather, but now there was little enemy resistance from land or air. Two attacks destroyed 158 planes in the air, on the ground, in their hangars and airfields and five small vessels were sunk. Numerous ground installations were attacked. Two aircraft plants were heavily damaged; radar installations, aircraft

231

hangars, and two trains were demolished. The ships of the task force suffered no damage during the attack.

Japanese airpower was at the ebb. The Imperial Japanese Navy as a fighting force was defeated, and the enemy was left with meager defenses of only land-based planes with poorly trained pilots resorting to kamikaze tactics.

On February 27, the *Santa Fe* and her group detached from the Tokyo invasion task force then headed back for Ulithi, anchoring there on March 1, 1945. The United States Navy was in charge, or so it seemed, of the seas around Japan.

MacArthur, still cleaning up at Luzon, prepared for the invasion of the Japanese mainland. It was estimated by the combined military staffs that it would take a million men to successfully take "the land of the rising sun." That buildup was taking place.

Okinawa Operation: Kyushu, Shikoku, and Rescue of USS Franklin

Kyushu: March 14-18, 1945

The capture of the Marianas and Philippines placed the Americans on a strategic line some 1500 miles from the Japanese homeland and across its direct routes of communication to the south. The occupation of Iwo Jima had advanced this line to within 640 miles of Tokyo.

The Joint Chiefs of Staff decided the next step was to secure a position in the Nansei Shoto chain, which extended in a shallow loop from Kyushu, the southernmost of the main Japanese islands, down to

Japanese held Formosa. Okinawa, the largest and most populous island in this chain, had numerous sites for airfields from which planes of almost any type could reach industrial Kyushu only 350 miles away, and attack the enemy's communications to Korea, to the Chinese mainland, and to the Indo-China and Singapore areas. Since Okinawa also had several excellent naval anchorages, it was chosen as the objective.

By March 1, 1945, the *Santa Fe* and her task group were anchored at Ulithi. Task Force 58 reorganized under Spruance's Fifth Fleet, with Admiral Mitscher in tactical command. The *"Lucky Lady"* was assigned to Task Group 58.2. On March 14, 1945, she sortied from Ulithi with her group en route for airstrikes on the Japanese Empire. Upon completion of training exercises, the fleet refueled on March 16 and began its approach on Kyushu.

On the morning of March 18, from a position about 125 miles southeast of Kyushu, the carriers launched strikes on that island in order to eliminate future airborne resistance to the Okinawa invasion forces. Enemy planes were in the area, and made minor attacks on other task groups, but none approached the *Santa Fe* and her unit closer than eight miles. After this attack, Task Group 58.2 retired to the southeast and around midnight, changed course to the north and began the approach toward Shikoku.

Shikoku Island and Rescue of USS Franklin: March 19 – 24, 1945

On March 19, 1945, fifty miles off the coast of Japan, *Santa Fe* and her fleet launched an air assault against Shikoku Island. At dawn the same morning, the carrier, USS *Franklin* (dubbed "*Big Ben*"), maneuvered close to the Japanese mainland and launched a fighter sweep against Honshu and later a strike against shipping in Kobe Harbor. Suddenly a Japanese bomber pierced the cloud cover, made a low level run, and rocketed over the bow of the 27,000-ton carrier, sweeping the length of her flight deck with two 500-pound bombs.

The first bomb struck near the *Franklin's* bridge. The second bomb smashed through the flight deck amidst her parked planes. The explosion rolled into one tremendous detonation. The *Franklin* turned out of the formation with her track marked by a trail of sailors bobbing in the water. Large bombs exploded, throwing men the length of the ship. The whole after end of her flight deck was engulfed in a mass of boiling flames and black smoke. To control the smoke, the Captain of the *Franklin* was steaming the only possible course, crosswind, and this was taking him straight to Japan.

Trailing this enormous blizzard of bombs, bullets, wood splinters, and jagged hunks of shrapnel was the cruiser *Santa Fe*. Captain Fitz had received orders to cover and assist the damaged *Franklin,* now dead in the water about 50 miles off the Japanese mainland. As Fitz and his crew approached the burning ship, they were haunted by memories of the fate of many crew members of the *Birmingham* (*Santa Fe*'s sister cruiser), who had been killed attempting to aid the damaged *Princeton* at the Battle of Leyte Gulf.

First to inch within touching distance of the *Franklin's* stricken sides was the destroyer *Miller*, who recovered some of the crew, then sped away to transfer them to another ship. While awaiting her turn, *Santa Fe* dropped over life nets, life jackets, and rafts to the men struggling in their carrier's wake. Captain Fitz took his cruiser close aboard the *Franklin* on the first pass in, while he sized up the situation.

In the words of the Assistant Damage Control Officer Lieutenant Chauncey B. King,

> *"We passed so close aboard that our after fire-fighting party was able to put out the fires in the Franklin's 40mm gun tubs with our hose lines. Twenty millimeter and forty millimeter ammunition were exploding and shooting all over the place. In fact, any time we approached closer than 1,000 yards we were showered with the carrier's projectiles."*

Santa Fe circled and moved in on the *Franklin's* starboard side, receiving the wounded by gangway and makeshift mailbag breeches—buoys for about 45 minutes until they were forced to cast off from the rapidly drifting carrier. Captain Fitz then brought the *Santa Fe* up to the *Franklin* at 25 knots, gave her a hard right rudder, and backed full on both engines. She stopped in the water a few feet off the *Franklin* for a perfect approach. Despite a 13-degree list, the carrier's heading was now fairly steady.

Captain Gehres of the *Franklin* later noted about the *Santa Fe*:

> *"Coming in at 25 knots at a wide angle, she slammed in against us and held the Franklin with her engines. It was*

the most daring piece of seamanship I ever saw. I want
to give the skipper full credit. It took a lot of nerve."

Now huddled along the carrier's leaning side, the *Santa Fe* passed hose lines over to pour water on the *Franklin's* blazing flight deck. With all phone, tube and speaker inter-communication dead on the *Franklin,* men fighting the fire in various parts of the ships were isolated from the bridge. With shrapnel sounding like hail on their helmets, *Santa Fe* signalmen filled the gap. Orders and reports passed from the after flight deck of the *Franklin* to men on the cruiser's fantail, relayed by phone to the signal bridge, and signaled by semaphore to the bridge of the *Franklin.* Below decks, teams were busy reinforcing the *Santa Fe's* hull plating with timbers and shoring to off-set the pressure of the sea grinding the cruiser against the sides and gun mounts of the carrier. In the *Santa Fe* sick bay, Medical Officer Lt. Commander Carl Gilman and his men pitched in on the task of treating the *Franklin's* wounded.

Franklin crew members continued to cross the thin valley separating the crashing, colliding ships via lines, radio masts, and a catwalk placed from the carrier's flight deck to the *Santa Fe's* No. 2 five-inch mount. To prevent them from catching fire from the *Franklin,* who continued to spew geysers of flame, the *Santa Fe's* Kingfishers were jettisoned.

Meanwhile, the *Pittsburgh* was busy getting the *Franklin* in tow. By noon of March 22, the *Pittsburgh* cast off the tow, and the *Franklin* steamed under her own power.

The *Santa Fe* crew operated alongside the burning *Franklin* for almost two hours, rescuing roughly half of the men from the carrier's burning hulk. The casualties on the *Franklin* totaled 724 killed or missing and 265 wounded. It would be recorded as one of the single, greatest disasters in the history of U.S. Naval warfare. The *Franklin* Rescue was *Santa Fe's* 55th mission since her original shakedown cruise in March 1943.

Secretary of the Navy, James Forrestal, awarded the *Santa Fe* and her crew, the Navy Unit Commendation, which read as follows:

"For exceptionally meritorious service in support of military operations on March 19, 1945. Promptly approaching the USS FRANKLIN after that vessel had been severely damaged by enemy aircraft, the USS SANTA FE heroically fought raging fires and put aboard rescue parties into the flaming hangars despite the serious hazards created by exploding gasoline, bombs and ammunition, in an effort to salvage the crippled carrier and save her stricken crew members. Within easy range of enemy air bases, she kept all guns manned and ready to repel any hostile attacks while lying close aboard the FRANKLIN's burning sides for a period of more than two hours to pick up isolated groups of wounded and trapped men. The valiant achievements of

the SANTA FE in saving many lives and aiding in the safe withdrawal of a valuable Fleet unit attest the professional skill and fearless devotion to duty of her officers and men, and reflect the highest credit upon the United States Naval Service."

The *Santa Fe* safely guided the *Franklin* and two other cripples to Ulithi, arriving March 24, 1945. On the 27th, she again left with the damaged *Franklin* and arrived at Pearl Harbor April 3. Upon her arrival, Commander-in-Chief of the Pacific Fleet, Admiral Nimitz, sent the following message to the *Franklin* and *Santa Fe*:

"It is evident that the return of the Franklin to port required skill and courage of the highest degree on the part of those who participated. The officers and men who returned on the Franklin and also the officers and men of the Santa Fe who rendered invaluable assistance have set a high standard of seamanship, courage and devotion to duty which will always be an inspiration to the Fleet. Well done to all hands."

Harold Fitz, *Santa Fe's* captain, was awarded the Navy Cross for his display of outstanding seamanship, ability, and daring in assisting the *Franklin*.

Santa Fe received her 14th and final Battle Star and Ridgeway his 16th and final Battle Star.

The remainder of *Franklin's* men came ashore, while *Santa Fe* and her crew headed on April 4, 1945 for Terminal Island Navy Yard at San Pedro, California. Upon arrival on April 10, the *Santa Fe* crew was welcomed by a familiar voice. Dinah Shore, in her famous Southern drawl, greeted the surprised sailors with a "Hiya, fellas!" and then began singing "Oh What a Beautiful Morning." After several more songs, the Hollywood star boarded the *Santa Fe*, kissed one of the sailor's hats, and began giving out autographs. Two weeks later, the *Santa Fe* men themselves became the stars of the popular Vox Pop radio program.

The *"Lucky Lady"* had now plied 221,750 engine miles of sea service since her commissioning and racked up 25 months of rigorous combat in the Pacific.

Santa Fe's worn out crew was granted a much deserved 30-day leave for rest and recuperation while the ship was completely re-gunned and her boilers and machinery given a major overhaul. New radar, fire control equipment and a radio coding machine were installed while the light cruiser was in dry dock at Terminal Island. Her bow was strengthened and four 40mm mounts added. Rear Admiral Deyo returned aboard, and *Santa Fe* was established as the flagship of Cruiser Division 14.

War's End: August 1, 1945 – January 26, 1946

Occupation of Japan

After a ten-day refresher training off San Clemente, *Santa Fe* was replenished with ammunition, stores, and fuel and departed San

Pedro for Pearl Harbor on July 2, 1945, fully expecting to spend another two years in the Pacific fight. But events were taking a dramatic turn. While the *Lucky Lady* practiced anti-aircraft exercises off Oahu on August 6, a B-29 bomber took off from Tinian Island, flew over Hiroshima, Japan, and dropped a single, atom bomb. Three days later, Nagasaki was bombed with another devastating single hit.

On August 12, *Santa Fe* sortied from Pearl Harbor with cruiser-carrier Task Group 12.3, including her old friend *Birmingham*. Three days later, the armada sailed from Pearl Harbor en route for an attack on Wake Island to the west. On August 15, 1945, the Japanese surrendered, and the task group diverted to Eniwetok arriving there August 19, 1945. From there, *Santa Fe* and a portion of her group proceeded to Okinawa and anchored peacefully in Buckner Bay, August 26, 1945, while the surrender pact was being signed in Tokyo Bay.

Surrender of Sasebo Naval Arsenal Aboard USS Santa Fe

At the peak of the war, the Imperial Japanese Navy employed some 50,000 workers at the Sasebo Naval Arsenal, constructing and refitting destroyers, light cruisers, submarines, and other war vessels. The 21st IJN Air Arsenal, established jointly at Sasebo and Omura, produced a total of 966 aircraft. The Sasebo base facilitated repairs on the battleships *Yamato* and *Musashi* during the Pacific War.

On September 20, 1945, Rear Admiral Morton L. Deyo, Commander of Task Force 55, whose flag flew on the *Santa Fe*, steamed into Sasebo port. On the evening of September 21, an occupation conference was held aboard the USS *Santa Fe*. Vice Admiral Sugiyama, Commander of the Sasebo Naval Arsenal, formally surrendered the Japanese base to Rear Admiral Deyo.

U. S. Marines began landing at various points throughout the Sasebo Harbor on September 22, 1945. By the end of the day, 10,000 troops safely landed.

The *Santa Fe* left Sasebo, October 8, but a typhoon forced her to stop at Nagasaki. My father told me of taking a tour through the bombed out area in a jeep. At that juncture, he truly knew the war was over.

The first port on Honshu to be visited was Wakayama. After a 24-hour stop, *Santa Fe* left for Yokosuka, located at the entrance to Tokyo Bay. With both Tokyo and Yokohama as liberty ports and the Emperor's palace, the Imperial Hotel, and the Ginza district nearby, there was abundant opportunity for sightseeing and souvenirs.

On October 17, 1945, the *Santa Fe* changed commanders and Captain James S. Freeman replaced Captain Fitz, with orders to sail to Ominato for duty as Flagship of Commander Northern Japan Area for the month ahead. During that time, *Santa Fe* anchored at Otaru, Hakodate, and Aomori during their occupations.

Magic Carpet Ride

On November 14, 1945, *Santa Fe* reported for "Magic Carpet" duty. Sailing south the next day to Saipan, she embarked high-point personnel and headed for the States. On her last "carpet ride" January 9, 1946, the *Lucky Lady* returned from Guam Island, packed to capacity with a load of grateful GIs.

Snow fell on the naval yard when the USS *Santa Fe* sailed into Bremerton, Washington on January 26, 1946.

CHAPTER TWENTY-ONE

RIDGEWAY MARRIES, LIFE AFTER THE WAR

E. J. Ridgeway Marries Sister of Santa Fe Gunner's Mate

Tim Haller was in E. J. Ridgeway's gunnery division on the USS *Santa Fe*. Haller was a big guy–six feet, eight inches tall. Upon arrival at Bremerton, Tim left the ship and went home for good. After all, the war was over—at least for Tim. It never occurred to the "absentee" sailor that he was now AWOL.

GM1/c Ridgeway, a pretty big fella himself—six feet, three inches tall—was ordered to bring Seaman Haller back to his ship. Tim was found living with his uncle and aunt, Bill and Dottie Delude, in Seattle where E. J. met Tim's sister, Lois. Ninety days later at the Bremerton Naval Chapel, E. J. Ridgeway and Lois Haller were married with full military honors.

My father served his remaining enlistment period aboard two ships, the USS *Canberra* (CL-70) and the USS *Quincy* (CA-71). In October of 1946, E. J. Ridgeway earned an honorable discharge from the United States Navy. He cleaned out his locker and shifted all belongings into his sea bag for the last time.

E. J. Ridgeway – Life after the war

A Return to "Spiritual Roots"

E. J. Ridgeway's spiritual roots were planted seven years before he was born on his grandfather's property in Snead, Alabama. Apparently, Hilliard ("Hill"), a long-time member of Ebenezer Methodist Church, was caught up in a Pentecostal revival that swept the hills of western North and South Carolina, east Tennessee, and Northeast Alabama. Several denominations sprung from it, and one of those was the Church of God headquartered in Cleveland, Tennessee.

"Hill" contacted the Alabama's State Overseer of the Churches of God and arranged to hold a tent revival on his property. The meeting was held in August 1915, and 13 charter members established the Mount Zion Church of God. Beginning in September, the new congregation held meetings in Hilliard and Octavia Ridgeway's home until a building was erected in 1917. Elliejay's (E.J.) mother, Georgia (Wright) Ridgeway, was one of the founding members.

The Ridgeway family's spiritual beliefs would have a profound influence in E. J.'s later years. What he experienced as a young boy in Northeast Alabama would change his life beginning in 1948.

When GM1/c Ridgeway was honorably discharged from the U.S. Navy in 1946, he and his wife, Lois, eventually moved back to Alabama and a couple of years later, they both were converted and became active members of the Church of God. Shortly thereafter, E. J. felt the call into the ministry. He and Lois moved to Cleveland, Tennessee where he attended Lee Bible College (now Lee University), affiliated with the Church of God, and became an ordained bishop at age 29.

After studying at Lee, the couple returned to Birmingham, where E. J. went to work at Anderson Electric Company. During this time, the Church of God state office planted a church in Gardendale, Alabama, on Fieldstown Road. E. J. was appointed as pastor, though he continued working at his job. The Ridgeways began a family as the small congregation grew, holding their services in a tent.

The sawdust on the ground was perfect for a small boy to play in during services, and the weather was always a factor. One Sunday was especially memorable. When the congregation arrived to worship, the pews were gone. Apparently, E. J. and another pastor, who had loaned the pews to the church, had a "miscommunication" so the pastor took the pews. The small congregation, undaunted by the lack of seating, held service anyway. E. J. determined it was time to build a sanctuary.

Brother Ridgeway located land and construction began. The church was (and still is) a cinder block building with the labor donated by the congregation.

E. J.'s relatives, the Painters, came down from Blount County and did the masonry work. The first service was proudly held before the floors were installed. From then on building would become an important skill in Pastor Ridgeway's life, work, and ministry.

Like George Bailey in "It's a Wonderful Life," Pastor Ridgeway wanted to provide affordable housing for the average working family. He became a state licensed contractor in Alabama and built several hundred homes (including more than one hundred FHA 235 and Farmers' Home Administration funded homes) as well as several churches and parsonages. He pastored for more than 40 years, serving eight Church of God congregations, and preached 3,777 sermons with 270 conversions and 275 members added to the church.

For 15 years, E. J. owned and operated Pathway Christian Bookstore in Midfield, Alabama. After his retirement in 1985, he took a renewed interest in his past Navy years, connecting with his former shipmates and attending reunions of both the USS *Vincennes* (CA-44) and USS *Santa Fe* (CL-60).

On April 2005, E.J. and Lois Haller Ridgeway celebrated their 59th wedding anniversary. Five months later, on September 28, 2005, E. J. Ridgeway passed away and was buried October 1st at Ebenezer Cemetery, Snead, Alabama, with full military and church honors.

E. J. RIDGEWAY OBITUARY

Birth: January 10, 1922

Death: September 28, 2005

Rev. E. J. Ridgeway, of McCalla, AL, passed away at the age of 83. He was born at Snead, AL. He retired from the ministry in 1985 after 40 years of serving a total of eight churches. He is survived by his wife, Lois, three children, three grandchildren and five great-grandchildren.

Ministry of E. J. Ridgeway:

First sermon - Empire Church of God – 1948

Attended Lee College (University) – 1948-1951

Built First Church – Fieldstown – pastored 1952-1955

Overton, Pastor – 1956-1959

Falkville, Pastor – 1959-1962

Evangelized – 1963

Moulton, Pastor – 1964-1973 – Built church and parsonage.

Roebuck (Sherwood Forest), Pastor – 1973-1974

Oneonta, Pastor – 1975-1976

Pratt Highway, Pastor – 1976-1977

Caffee Junction – 1977-1985. Built a fellowship hall onto existing church, built new parsonage prior to initiating construction of new church.

Retired: 1985

Regular monthly speaker at Tannehill Park Church since 1978.

BIBLIOGRAPHY

Alexander, Joseph H. Col. (2013), Across *the Reef: The Marine Assault of Tarawa,* CreateSpace Independent Publishing Platform (January 17, 2013)

Bix, Herbert P. (2001), *Hirohito and the Making of Modern Japan.* New York: Perennial / Harper Collins Publishers

Budiansky, Stephen (2000). *Battle of Wits: The Complete Story of Codebreaking in World War II,* Budiansky, Touchstone (Simon & Schuster, Inc.)

Carson, Elliot (2013). *Joe Rochefort's War: The Odyssey of the Codebreaker Who Outwitted Yamamoto at Midway,* Naval Institute Press, Reprint Edition, (September 15, 2013)

Clayton KS Chung (2006), *The Doolittle Raid 1942* Oxford UK: Osprey Publishing

Cray, Ed, (1990) General *of the Army: George C. Marshall, Soldier and Statesman*, Cooper Square Press, An Imprint of Rowan & Littlefield Publishing Group, New York, New York.

Cutler, Thomas (1994). *The Battle of Leyte Gulf: 23-26 October 1994.* Annapolis, Maryland, U.S.: Naval Institute Press.

Doolittle, Gen. James H. "Jimmy" (1991), *I Could Never Be So Lucky Again,* New York: Bantam Books

Dorris, Jonathan Truman (1947). *A Log of the Vincennes*, Standard Printing Company, Louisville, KY, 1947

Evan, Thomas (2006). *Sea of Thunder: Four Commanders and the Last Great Naval Campaign, 1941-45,"* New York: Simon & Schuster

Fahey, James J. (1963). *Pacific War Diary*, Zebra Books, New York: Kensington Publishing Corp.

Glines, Carroll V. (1988). *The Doolittle Raid*, New York: Orion Books

Green, Michael (1996). *MacArthur in the Pacific,* Osceola, WI: Motorbooks, International

Hall, R.Cargill (1991). *Lightning Over Bougainville – The Yamamoto Mission Reconsidered,* Smithsonian Institution Press

Hammel, Eric and Lane, John (1980). *76 Hours: Invasion of Tarawa,* New York: Tower Books

Hornfischer, James D. (2005). *Last Stand of the Tin Can Sailors,* New York: Bantam Books

Hornfischer, James D. (2011). *Neptune's Inferno,* Bantam Books, an imprint of Random House, Inc., New York (Page 91)

Hoyt, Edwin P. (1972). *The Battle of Leyte Gulf: The Death Knell of the Japanese Fleet,* New York: Weybright and Talley.

Hoyt, Edwin P. (1994). *Closing the Circle: War in the Pacific: 1945,* Avon Books.

Jackson, Steve (2003). *Lucky Lady: The World War II Heroics of the USS Santa Fe and Franklin,* Carroll & Graf Publishers

Kelly, Orr (1991). *Hornet Inside Story of the F/A-18, Airlife Publishing Ltd.*

Lawson, Ted W., Capt. (2004), *Thirty Seconds Over Tokyo,* Bronx, New York: Ishi Press International.

Manchester, William (1978). *American Caesar: Douglas MacArthur 1880-1964,* Little Brown & Company, Boston, Toronto

Mooney, James L. (1981). *Dictionary of American Naval Fighting Ships, Vol III,* Naval history division, Dept. Of the Navy, P. 527-530.

Morison, Samuel E. (2001), *"Aleutians, Gilberts and Marshalls, June 1942-April 1944,"* History of United States Naval Operations in World War II, Castle Books

Morison, Samuel E. (1956). *"Leyte, June 1944-January 1945,"* History of United States Naval Operations in World War II, XII, Boston: Little Brown & Company.

Morison, Samuel E. (1963). *Two-Ocean War,* Canada: Little, Brown & Company LTD.

Morison, Samuel E. (1958). *Leyte June 1944-January 1945.* Annapolis, Md., Naval Institute Press, Pg. 172

Nelson, Craig (2002). *The First Heroes: The Extraordinary Story of the Doolittle Raid—America's First World War II Victory*; Penguin Books

Parshall, Jonathan; Tully, Anthony (2005). *Shattered Sword: The Untold Story of the Battle of Midway.* Dulles, Virginia: Potomac Books

Potter, E. B; Nimitz, Chester W. (1960). *Sea Power: A Naval History.* Prentice-Hall Englewood Cliffs, New Jersey.

Prange, Gordon W. (1983). *Miracle at Midway,* Penguin Books/McGraw-Hill Book Company, New York

Reynolds, Clark (1968). *The Fast Carriers.* U.S. Naval Institute Press.

Ruiz, Kenneth C., USN (Ret.) (2005). *The Luck of the Draw,* Zenith Press, an imprint of MBI Publishing Company, St. Paul, MN

Schwyhart, Robert Marion, Captain, USN (Ret.) (Oral History Program) (1984). Chaplain Corps History Branch, Office of the Chief Chaplains, Dept. Of the Navy

Scott, James M. (2015). *Target Tokyo: Jimmy Doolittle and the Raid that Avenged Pearl Harbor,"* W. W. Norton & Co.

Symonds, Craig L. (2011). *The Battle of Midway,* Oxford University Press, New York

Taylor, Theodore (1954). *The Magnificent Mitscher.* Naval Institute Press.

Toll, Ian W. (2012). *Pacific Crucible: War at Sea in the Pacific, 1941-1942,* W. W. Norton & Company

Touhy, William (2007). *America's Fighting Admirals,* Zenith Press, an imprint of MBI Publishing Company LLC

Wilmont, H.P. (2005). *The Battle of Leyte Gulf: The Last Fleet Action (Twentieth-Century Battles),* Indiana University Press,

Woodward, C. Vann (1947). *The Battle of Leyte Gulf: The Incredible Story of World War II's Largest Naval Battle,* New York: McMillan

REFERENCE NOTES

CHAPTER ONE - Neutrality Patrols and Gold Runs

USS *Vincennes* CA-44 – Background -
www.historycentral.com/navy/cruiser/Vincennes.html

USS *Vincennes* CA-44 – Fact Index - www.fact-index.com/u/us/uss_vincennes__ca_44_.html

Naval History and Heritage Command – *Vincennes* II (CA-44) -
www.history.navy.mil/research/histories/ship-histories/danfs/v/vincennes-ii.html

First Gold Run:
The Official Chronology of the U.S. Navy in WW2 by Robert J. Cressman, Contemporary History Branch Naval Historical Center, 1999 (French Gold)
archive.org/stream/TheOfficialChronologyOfTheUSNavyInWorldWarII/TheOfficialChronologyOf
TheUSNavyInWorldWarII_djvu.txt

Second Gold Run:
HyperWar – The Official Chronology of the US Navy in World War II – Chapter III: 1941; March 17, 20, 1941 and April 16, 1941.
www.ibiblio.org/hyperwar/USN/USN-Chron/USN-Chron-1941.html

World War 2 Database – USS *Vincennes* -
ww2db.com/ship_spec.php?ship_id=302

Historical event dates - Chronology of International Events, 1938-1941
faculty.virginia.edu/setear/students/fdrneutr/38%20to%2041%20Alt.htm

Winston Sail 12X Convoy (Task Force 14) -
www.cofepow.org.uk/pages/ships_convoy_william_sail.htm

Ghost Ships – The Unknown Pre-War US Navy Globe-Circling Voyage – Jerome O'Connor, July 1, 2002 - historyarticles.com/ghost-ships/

CHAPTER TWO - U.S. Task Force 14 and Secret William Sail 12x (WS 12x) Convoy

Cofepow-Ships-Convoy William Sail -
www.cofepow.org.uk/pages/ships_convoy_william_sail.htm

Secret Mission to Singapore: Proceedings, July 2002, Jerome M. O'Connor – Military.Com
www.military.com/Content/MoreContent1?file=NI_Singapore

Reference to *Vincennes* sailor's appendectomy - Cofepow-Ships-Convoy William Sail -
www.cofepow.org.uk/pages/ships_convoy_william_sail.htm

Naval History and Heritage Command – Vincennes II (CA-44)
www.history.navy.mil/research/histories/ship-histories/danfs/v/vincennes-ii.html

Winston Sail 12x Convoy (Task Force 14) -
www.cofepow.org.uk/pages/ships_convoy_william_sail.htm

Secret Mission to Singapore: Proceedings, July 2002, Jerome M. O'Connor
www.military.com/Content/MoreContent1?file=NI_Singapore

References to British Navy Discovers German "Ultra" and "Enigma"
www.cofepow.org.uk/pages/ships_convoy_william_sail.htm

CHAPTER THREE – America Declares War

Winston Sail 12x Convoy (Task Force 14) -
www.cofepow.org.uk/pages/ships_convoy_william_sail.htm

Secret Mission to Singapore: Proceedings, July 2002, Jerome M. O'Connor

"Admiral Sir Dudley Pound phoned news of the disaster to Churchill" .... *Finest Hour Prince of Wales and Repulse: Churchill's "Veiled Threat" Reconsidered*, Churchill Proceedings, 2007, Barry Gough - www.winstonchurchill.org/publications/finest-hour/finest-hour-139/prince-of-wales-and-repulse-churchills-veiled-threat-reconsidered

Naval History and Heritage Command – Vincennes II (CA-44)
www.history.navy.mil/research/histories/ship-histories/danfs/v/vincennes-ii.html

References to Chaplain Schwyhart
Schwyhart, Robert Marion, Captain, USN (Ret.) (Oral History Program) (1984). Chaplain Corps History Branch, Office of the Chief Chaplains, Dept. Of the Navy

CHAPTER FOUR - America Prepares to Strike Back

USS *Enterprise* CV6-The Most Decorated Ship of the Second World War – Website – The Doolittle Raid: April 18, 1942 www.cv6.org/1942/doolittle/doolittle_2.htm

North American B-25 Mitchell - acepilots.com/planes/b25.html

Treasure Island Fair/Golden Gate International Exposition, Historical Essay, Gail Hynes Shea
www.foundsf.org/index.php?title=Treasure_Island_Fair: Golden_Gate_International_Exposition

Web Article: The Story of Treasure Island, Part 1, Richard Miller aka "Sparkletack"
www.treasureislandfestival.com/2010/island.php

"On September 29, 1940, the lights of the Golden Gate..."
Web Article: The Story of Treasure Island, Part 1, Richard Miller aka "Sparkletack" - www.treasureislandfestival.com/2010/island.php

CHAPTER FIVE – The Doolittle Raid

World War II Database – Doolittle Raid, 18 Apr 1942 – C. Peter Chen - ww2db.com/battle_spec.php?battle_id=26

CHAPTER SIX – Coral Sea and Prelude to Midway

The Battle of the Coral Sea - Pacific Aviation Museum – Florida Island, Hawaii – Posted March 14, 2014
www.pacificaviationmuseum.org/pearl-harbor-blog/battle-of-the-coral-sea

CHAPTER SEVEN – Battle of Midway

Order of Battle en.wikipedia.org/wiki/Battle_of_Midway

Naval History Blog – U.S. Naval Institute – *Admiral Nimitz and the Battle of Midway – June 3-6, 1942* - Friday, June 3, 2011 by Naval Institute Archives

C. Wade McClusky, LCDR Wade McClusky - www.cv6.org/company/accounts/wmcclusky/

CHAPTER EIGHT – Guadalcanal Campaign (August 7, 1942 – February 9, 1943)

Opening Salvos: The Battle of Savo Island, August 9, 1972 Prologue, Battle, Epilogue
www.microworks.net/pacific/battles/savo_island.htm

Long Lance vs. Mark 15
www.quora.com/In-World-War-II-between-Germany-or-Japan-which-had-the-better-torpedoes

The Freeper Foxhole Revisits the Battle of Savo Island -
www.freerepublic.com/focus/f-vetscor/1480729/posts

Disaster at Savo Island, 1942 by Lieutenant Colonel David E. Quantock, United States Army

References to Chaplain Schwyhart - Schwyhart, Robert Marion, Captain, USN (Ret.) (Oral History Program) (1984). Chaplain Corps History Branch, Office of the Chief Chaplains, Dept. Of the Navy

Operation Watchtower: The Battle for Guadalcanal (August 1942 – February 1943)
www.historyofwar.org/articles/battles_guadalcanal.html#intro

CHAPTER NINE – Disaster at Savo Island August 9, 1942

Opening Salvos: The Battle of Savo Island, August 9, 1972 Prologue, Battle, Epilogue
www.microworks.net/pacific/battles/savo island.htm

Disaster at Savo Island, 1942 by Lieutenant Colonel David E. Quantock, United States Army
www.ibiblio.org/hyperwar/USN/rep/Savo/Quantock/

CHAPTER TEN – USS *Vincennes* Sinks

Opening Salvos: The Battle of Savo Island, August 9, 1972 Prologue, Battle, Epilogue
www.microworks.net/pacific/battles/savo island.htm

Disaster at Savo Island, 1942 by Lieutenant Colonel David E. Quantock, United States Army
www.ibiblio.org/hyperwar/USN/rep/Savo/Quantock/

"For our first two hours in the water…"
Joe Fritcher – Gunner's Mate First Class (GM1/c), U.S. Navy, WWII
www.gabc.org/assets/docs/veterans/fritcherjoe.pdf

Japanese firing records
Abstract of *"Disaster at Savo Island, 1942"* by Lieutenant Colonel
David E. Quantock, United States Army, USAWC Class of 2002,
U.S. Army War College, Carlisle Barracks, PA

Burial at Sea - U.S. Navy Burial at Sea - www.military.com/navy-
birthday/us-navy-burial-at-sea.html

Internment on Treasure Island
Iron Bottom Sound – The Battle of Savo Island 9 August, 1942 -
USS *Astoria* CA-34 – The Official Home of 'Nasty Asty' – Brent
Jones - www.ussastoria.org/Iron_Bottom_Sound.html, Visited
6/26/2016.

CHAPTER ELEVEN - USS *Santa Fe* (CL-60) - The *"Lucky Lady"*

Launching - USS *Santa Fe* Cruise Record – Pg. 18

Aleutian Operation - USS *Santa Fe* Cruise Record – Pgs. 20-23

Aleutian Islands Campaign - en.wikipedia.org/wiki/Aleutian
Islands Campaign

Launch and Aleutians - USS *Santa Fe* – 1942-46 –
usssantafe.net/Docs/launch and aleutians.htm

**Office of the Historian – Milestones: 1937-1945 – The
Casablanca Conference, 1943** history.state.gov/milestones/1937-
1945/casablanca

CHAPTER TWELVE - Nimitiz Island Hopping Strategy/The Pacific Raids

USS *Santa Fe* – 1942-46 – usssantafe.net/docs/pacific raids,
treasury-bougainville, and the gilberts.htm

Pacific Raids - USS *Santa Fe* Cruise Record – Pgs. 28-29, 34
Bougainville Night Attack - USS *Santa Fe* Cruise Record – Pg. 36

"This would make *The Birmingham* a one-ocean Navy..." - USS *Santa Fe* – 1942-46
usssantafe.net/docs/pacific raids, treasury-bougainville, and the gilberts.htm

CHAPTER THIRTEEN - Tarawa Invasion

Gilbert Islands Operation: Tarawa Invasion - USS *Santa Fe* Cruise Record – Pgs. 39-41

Naval Gunfire Support of Amphibious Operations: Past, Present, and Future – Donald M. Weller, Major General, USMC (Retired) – Prepared for Naval Sea Systems Command Headquarters, U.S. Marine Corps – Naval Surface Weapons Center – Dahlgren, Virginia 22448 – Received March 28, 1978.

Battle of Tarawa Facts – www.worldwar2facts.org/battle-of-tarawa.html

CHAPTER FOURTEEN - Marshall Islands Operations and Asiatic-Pacific Raids

The Marshalls - USS *Santa Fe* Cruise Record – pgs. 42-45

Marshall Islands Campaign – 29 Jan 1944 – 21 Feb 1944 – C. Peter Chen, WW2 Database

The National WWII Museum – New Orleans – Focus on: D-Day Kwajalein
www.nationalww2museum.org/see-hear/collections/focus-on/d-day-kwajalein.html

Caroline Islands – en.wikipedia.org

"The Raid on Truk Lagoon," Roger D. McGrath, February 11, 2011, *The New American*

"Attack on Truk, Feb 16 – 18, 1944." C. Peter Chen, WW 2 Database

Fast Carrier Task Force – en.wikipedia.org/wiki/Fast Carrier Task Force

Naval Gunfire Support of Amphibious Operations: Past, Present, and Future – Donald M. Weller, Major General, USMC (Ret'd) – Prepared for Naval Sea Systems Command Headquarters, U.S. Marine Corps – Naval Surface Weapons Center – Dahlgreen, Virginia 22448 – Received March 28, 1978.

Naval Operations in the Pacific from March 1944 to October 1945 - Excerpted from Admiral Earnest J. King, *Second Report to the Secretary of the Navy: Covering Combat Operations from 1 March 1944 to 1 March, 1945.* March 1945, pp. 103-133 and *Second Report to the Secretary of the Navy: Covering the period 1 March 1945 to 1 October 1945.* December 1945, pp. 173-204] Combat Operations

Truk, Saipan Airstrikes - USS *Santa Fe* Cruise Record – pgs. 47-49

New Guinea (MacArthur) - USS *Santa Fe* Cruise Record – pgs. 51-53

CHAPTER FIFTEEN - Pacific Raids/1st Battle of Philippine Sea

Alfred L. Castle: *"President Roosevelt and General MacArthur at the Honolulu Conference 1944"*, The Hawaiian Journal of History, Volume 38. Alfred L. Castle is the Executive Director of the Samuel N. and Mary Castle Foundation

Alfred Thayer Mahan – Encyclopedia.com - www.encyclopedia.com/topic/Alfred_Thayer_Mahan.aspx

Battle of the Philippine Sea – Conservapedia www.conservapedia.com/Battle_of_the_Philippine_Sea

Navy's Two Platoon System - Intrepid Sea, Air & Space Museum – *"This Month in Intrepid's History,"* posted 8/21/14 www.intrepidmuseum.org/LatestNews/August-2014/This-Month-in-Intrepid

Naval Operations in the Pacific from March 1944 to October 1945
Excerpted from Admiral Earnest J. King, *Second Report to the Secretary of the Navy: Covering Combat Operations from 1 March 1944 to 1 March, 1945.* March 1945, pp. 103-133 and *Second Report to the Secretary of the Navy: Covering the period 1 March 1945 to 1 October 1945.* December 1945, pp. 173-204] Combat Operations

CHAPTER SIXTEEN - Western Caroline Islands Operations

Naval Operations in the Pacific from March 1944 to October 1945
Excerpted from Admiral Earnest J. King, *Second Report to the Secretary of the Navy: Covering Combat Operations from 1 March 1944 to 1 March, 1945.* March 1945, pp. 103-133 and *Second Report to the Secretary of the Navy: Covering the period 1 March 1945 to 1 October 1945.* December 1945, pp. 173-204] Combat Operations USS *Santa Fe* Cruise Record – Pgs. 54-55

Summer Offensive - USS *Santa Fe* Cruise Record – Pgs. 56-61

"Peleliu: The Forgotten Battle," Article by Major Henry J. Donigan – Originally published September 1994, Marine Corps, www.mca-marines.org/leatherneck/peleliu-forgotten-battle

Occupation of Palau - USS *Santa Fe* Cruise Record – Pgs. 65-67

Philippine Softening Up - USS *Santa Fe* Cruise Record – Pgs. 68-74

Second Battle of Philippines - USS *Santa Fe* Cruise Record – Pgs. 75-77

CHAPTER SEVENTEEN - Battle of Leyte Gulf

Naval Operations in the Pacific from March 1944 to October 1945
Excerpted from Admiral Earnest J. King, *Second Report to the Secretary of the Navy: Covering Combat Operations from 1 March 1944 to 1 March, 1945.* March 1945, pp. 103-133 and *Second Report to the Secretary of the Navy: Covering the period 1 March 1945 to 1 October 1945.* December 1945, pp. 173-204] Combat Operations

Battle of Leyte Gulf - en.wikipedia.org/wiki/Battle of Leyte Gulf

The Battle for Leyte Gulf – 23-26 October 1944 –
www.angelfire.com/fm/odyssey/leytegulf.htm

Performance of US Battleships at Surigao Strait by Joseph Czarnecki, Updated 30 April 2002
www.navweaps.com/index tech/tech-079.htm

CHAPTER EIGHTEEN – Battles off Samar and Cape Engaño

"...known as the "three taffies," because of their radio call sign." - Photographs of Task Unit 77.4.3 Including Specifications & Histories – USS *Heerman* (DD-532), CDR Amos T. Hathaway, USN, Commanding Officer – Leyte/Gulf Samar, October 17-25, 1944, www.bosamar.com/pages/dd532

Battle Off Samar 25 October 1944 – Destroyer History Foundation - destroyerhistory.org/actions/index.asp?pid=4583

"Johnston's gunnery officer, Lt. Robert C. Hagen...."
Photographs of Task Unit 77.4.3 Including Specifications & Histories – USS *Heerman* (DD-532), CDR Amos T. Hathaway, USN, Commanding Officer – Leyte/Gulf Samar, October 17-25, 1944, www.bosamar.com/pages/dd532

"In no engagement in its entire history...." Morison, Samuel E. (1956). *"Leyte, June 1944-January 1945,"* History of United States

Naval Operations in World War II, Volume XII, Boston: Little Brown & Company.

Santa Fe's **Actions – Oct. 23 & 25, 1944/Nov & Dec. Strikes –** USS *Santa Fe* Cruise Record - 78-79

The Pacific War Online Encyclopedia – Cape Engaño – pwencycl.kgbudge.com/C/a/Cape Engano.htm

CHAPTER NINETEEN - Luzon and East Leyte Strikes

Naval Operations in the Pacific from March 1944 to October 1945
Excerpted from Admiral Earnest J. King, *Second Report to the Secretary of the Navy: Covering Combat Operations from 1 March 1944 to 1 March, 1945.* March 1945, pp. 103-133 and *Second Report to the Secretary of the Navy: Covering the period 1 March 1945 to 1 October 1945.* December 1945, pp. 173-204] Combat Operations

Naval Gunfire Support of Amphibious Operations: Past, Present, and Future – Donald M. Weller, Major General, USMC (Ret'd) – Prepared for Naval Sea Systems Command Headquarters, U.S. Marine Corps – Naval Surface Weapons Center – Dahlgreen, Virginia 22448 – Received March 28, 1978.

Santa Fe Cruise Record – Pgs. 78, 79, 80, 88, 93-97.

CHAPTER TWENTY - Tokyo Raid/Okinawa/Rescue of USS *Franklin*

USS *Franklin* (CV-13) – Remembering Big Ben – www.ussfranklin.org/?page id=2

Rescue of the *Franklin* – USSsantafe.net/docs/iwojima_and_okinawa.htm

Rescue of the *Franklin* – USS Santa Fe Cruise Record – Pgs. 98-105

Naval Operations in the Pacific from March 1944 to October 1945 - Excerpted from Admiral Earnest J. King, *Second Report to the Secretary of the Navy: Covering Combat Operations from 1 March 1944 to 1 March, 1945.* March 1945, pp. 103-133 and *Second Report to the Secretary of the Navy: Covering the period 1 March 1945 to 1 October 1945.* December 1945, pp. 173-204] Combat Operations

Naval Gunfire Support of Amphibious Operations: Past, Present, and Future – Donald M. Weller, Major General, USMC (Retired) – Prepared for Naval Sea Systems Command Headquarters, U.S. Marine Corps – Naval Surface Weapons Center – Dahlgreen, Virginia 22448 – Received March 28, 1978.

For exceptionally meritorious service in support of military operations on March 19, 1945
usssantafe.net/docs/war's end.htm

USS *SANTA FE* – History Central –
www.historycentral.com/navy/MISC2/santafe.html

Sasebo Naval Arsenal – en.wikipedia.org/wiki/Sasebo Naval Arsenal

Sasebo Occupation – usssantafe.net/Docs/occupation.htm

www.ingramcontent.com/pod-product-compliance
Lightning Source LLC
LaVergne TN
LVHW051459080426
835509LV00017B/1831